For the Write Reason

31 Writers, Agents and Editors Share
Their Experiences With
Christian Publishing

MARYBETH WHALEN
GENERAL EDITOR

For the
Write Reason

31 Writers, Agents and Editors Share
Their Experiences With
Christian Publishing

UpWrite Books
A Division of WINEPRESS PUBLISHING

UpWrite Books (a division of WinePress Publishing, PO Box 428, Enumclaw, WA 98022) functions only as book publisher. As such, the ultimate design, content, editorial accuracy, and views expressed or implied in this work are those of the author.

ISBN 1-4141-0432-4
Library of Congress Catalog Card Number: 2005902972

Acknowledgements

· ·

To my Abba Father: Psalm 16:2, "I said to the Lord, You are my Lord; apart from You I have no good thing."

To my contributors: Thank you for believing in this project, encouraging me, praying for me, and giving of your time and wisdom to make this book possible. Psalm 16:3, "As for the saints who are in the land, they are the glorious ones in whom is all my delight."

To my husband Curt: Thank you for believing in me, loving me and supporting me. I am blessed among women. Additionally, a public thank you for keeping the children, helping me with computer issues, overlooking the state of the house, and eating out without complaining!

To my children: Jack, Ashleigh, Matthew, Rebekah, Bradley and the "player to be named later," you are my greatest credentials!

To Lysa TerKeurst: This book would never have happened without you serving as my head cheerleader. Your friendship means so much to me.

To my mom, Sandy Brown: All those years of reading to me, using big words with me, and making me believe I could do anything are represented in this book. I love you!

To the staff at Proverbs 31 Ministries: What a great bunch of ladies you are! Your contributions are making a difference in so many lives, including mine. Thank you for supporting this project and making it possible.

To Athena Dean and WinePress Publishing: You made this process painless and even fun! Thank you for catching the vision from the very beginning, and for answering my thousands of questions. You have been a joy to work with!

How to Use This Book

● ●

This book was created out of my own personal desire to learn from and be encouraged by other writers. As I entered the unique world of Christian publishing, God allowed specific people to come alongside me and walk me through what can be an overwhelming and daunting process. I was grateful for their wisdom and willingness to share their experience with a novice writer like myself. And then one day, the thought occurred to me—what do writers do who do not have these people in their lives? I pondered what a lonely, complicated process this would have been without them. I thanked the Lord for these people in my life and promised Him that I would, in turn, help any other writers He placed in my path in the future.

For the Write Reason became the answer to and fulfillment of that simple prayer. God laid this book on my heart and brought specific contributors into the project through His sovereignty, designing an amazing resource for Christian writers as only He could. This book is a way for you to learn the ins and outs of the Christian publishing world and glean from the wisdom of experienced professionals who already know the terrain. As you read their stories, you will share in their triumphs and frustrations, glimpse their passion for sharing God's Truth with others, and probably see much of yourself reflected in their words.

The book is written in a 31-day format with the idea being that, in the course of one month, you can read one profile and one Bible study each day. Through the profiles, you will be challenged, informed, and inspired by these very special contributors. It is likely that you will feel that you have made some new friends by the time you finish the book!

The camaraderie generated throughout the book is there to help you feel a connection with other Christian writers, since writing itself is such a solitary effort.

Through the Bible study, you will be able to connect even further with the Source of your inspiration. After you have heard others' stories, it is time to dig deeper into your own by hearing what God has to say to you personally through His Word. The purpose of the Bible study is to help you determine God's specific purpose for your writing. Where are you headed? Who are you seeking to glorify? What is your passion? Why has God called you for such a time as this? The goal of the Bible study is to enable you to get before God and really determine the answers to these and other questions. I highly recommend keeping a journal to record all that God reveals to you as you go through this book. I have even suggested some journal activities to get you thinking.

I have no doubt that God will use you for His kingdom. I am excited to see how He will use this book in your life. God loves you and wants you to hear His voice cheering you on as you seek to share what He has done in your life through your writing. If God uses this book to confirm His calling, challenge your outlook, or unveil something unexpected in your life, I would love to hear about it. Please email me at *Marybeth@proverbs31.org* to share your own stories. Many blessings to you as you seek to glorify God and perpetuate His Word!

Table of Contents

* *

All Bible Studies written by Marybeth Whalen

Dear Sami ~
Chase your dreams and
honor God! ♡ Lysa

God's Dreams for Me

• •

By: Lysa TerKeurst

I felt so insignificant as I made my way up to the speaker in the front of the room. She was surrounded by women of all ages. Some just wanted to give her a tearful hug. Others held her book in their hands looking for a note of encouragement and an autograph. I just wanted to ask her how? How do I take a broken life and allow God to use it for His glory? Is it possible that a girl rejected by her earthly father could actually be chosen and set apart for a divine calling? How did I get past the place of not even being able to make it through the day to proclaiming God's love from the podium?

I waited in line until it was my turn. Then as I opened my mouth to speak, my throat tightened, my eyes filled with tears, and all I could squeak out was an emotional, *how.* I wanted her to take me home with her and teach me. I wanted her to pack me in her suitcase and whisk me away from my life and into the life of one making a difference. I wanted her to share some quick-and-easy answer, a "step one-two-three and then you'll have the life you dream of, all for the low price of attending my seminar," type answer. But she wasn't a magician, or a slick salesman, or a woman looking for a new houseguest. She was a woman who'd experienced deep hurts and bitter disappointments, chosen to surrender her life to God and was now being used by Him.

She did not give me the quick, easy answer I was looking for. She didn't give me any profound wisdom or direction. A simple answer of how she got started was all my time in line allowed and then I found myself making my way back to my seat. But I wasn't heading back empty and without hope. What this speaker lacked in words she more than made up for in example. I had seen Jesus in her. I had seen living proof of God's redemption. I thought to myself, *If God could do that with her, there's hope for me after all.* The birth of something new, big and God-directed was revealed to me and confirmed in my heart in an undeniable way that day.

Things did not happen magically and immediately. There was a waiting period, a time of growth, development and perseverance that I had to go through for God to get me ready. There were lessons on patience, trust, surrender, letting go, and learning to take hold, that had to go before I stepped out. But even in this seemingly ineffective time of pruning and trials, God was preparing me for a season to come. This was not a waste of time. This "getting ready" period was an important part of fulfilling my calling. Though I couldn't see much fruit, God was getting my vine ready and healthy enough to be able to hold all He knew was coming.

I left the conference that day excited, only to be hit with Satan's attack. *Who do you think you are? Do you really think God could use a woman like you to help others?* Satan's whispers were relentless. At the conference, I had felt such assurance of God's calling but back in the midst of everyday life, I doubted. I got down on my knees and cried out to the Lord for His assurance and He met me at my point of need. God assured me that He doesn't call the qualified but He qualifies those He calls.

I always thought to be in ministry meant painting the facade that I was perfect, then I would be a qualified servant of God. I quickly learned that people aren't impressed with fake perfection, they're turned off and intimidated by it! God wanted me to be honest and real. He wanted to shine His grace, mercy, love, and redemption through my faults, failures, and frailties. He wanted to make me strong with His strength. He wanted to take credit for any and all good that would come from my ministry efforts.

As my ministry and speaking opportunities grew, I eventually got the bright idea to write a book. I typed out my speaking outlines in chapter form, thought of some catchy chapter titles, slapped a cover sheet on the rag-tag collection and called it a book proposal. A friend of mine and I naively headed to the Christian Booksellers Association convention fully expecting to find publishers. After all the hardest part to getting a book published was getting it written, right? Well, I quickly learned that couldn't be further from the truth. The wave of rejection letters that littered my desk in the months that followed the conference dashed my great hopes and big dreams.

God did have a plan for me and opened other doors to write smaller articles for newsletters and magazines. The first time I saw my name as the author of a published article, I knew. God might as well have opened the doors to the library and told me to count them if I could, for that's the number of books that would eventually come from my ministry to women. Not that I'd write them all but that women throughout the world would catch a vision for writing their messages and that I could have a part in giving them the courage to do so. I believed that God would one day give me the chance to write a book and I committed to wait on him. I would no longer go chasing after publishers, I would wait until God brought one to me. I took my book proposals, placed them in a file, closed the drawer and thanked God in advance for what would one day come to pass. I believed.

Three years later, I wrote an article for a financial publication. To be completely honest, I thought it was one of the worst articles I'd ever written. But the article made its way into a publisher's hands. He read it, loved it, and offered me a book contract. Only God could do such a thing! I think God wanted to make sure I knew that my getting a book contract had a lot less to do with me and a lot more to do with Him working through me—in His timing.

I was doing the happy dance everywhere I went. God did it! God really did it! I don't think my feet hit the ground for days. I was going to be a published author. I was thrilled beyond belief until a stark reality hit me: it's one thing to get a book contract but it's a whole different thing to actually write the book . . . all fifty thousand words of it. Was I nuts? Why did I want this, could someone please remind me? Do I know 50,000 words? Do I even know 1,000 words that I could somehow tangle together fifty different ways?

Though I was scared and unsure, I started gathering quotes and stories. I assumed a most authoritative writing voice and mechanically typed out my first 10,000 words. I sat back in sheer delight realizing I would make my editor's first deadline. I was to send this first section of the book off to her for approval before continuing on. Like a proud mama of a newborn baby, I nervously let someone else hold my little darling. I couldn't wait to hear her glowing report of how beautiful and full of promise my words were. Instead, I got back a two-page corrections sheet that could basically be summed up with two earth-shattering words, "Start over!"

I got down on my floor beside my computer, buried my face into the carpet, and wept out loud. I cried out to God. On the day I stood before the altar holding my dying dream, I realized I had two choices. I could demand to keep the dream for myself and smother it to certain death in my closed fist or I could hand it to the Resurrector. I placed my book in God's hands and only then did I understand. I did not have to sacrifice my entire book, I only had to lay it on the altar and leave it in God's hands.

God did require a sacrifice, but it was not the entire book project. My sacrifice was my first 10,000 words. The reward was a book re-worked where I found my place as my reader's friend rather than an official sounding expert.

Because I was willing to leave my plans behind, God let me participate in His. Looking back, I wouldn't have wanted it any other way. I still remember holding that first published book in my hands. Seeing my name on the cover, leafing through the pages, and seeing God's fingerprints all over this project brought tears to my eyes. Once again, I was reminded that the book was not really about getting a book published. That was just an aside, a fringe benefit. The real treasure was walking with God through the project. Being reminded first-hand that God does indeed have a plan. Not just a good plan. Not even a really good plan. God has the perfect plan.

Taken in part from Lysa TerKeurst's book "What Happens When Women Walk in Faith," copyright 2005, Harvest House Publishers.

Lysa TerKeurst is a wife, mother of five blessings named Jackson, Mark, Hope, Ashley and Brooke, and President of Proverbs 31 Ministries. She is the co-host of the ministry's national radio program which airs daily across the nation and abroad. Lysa is the award-winning author of several books, including *Radically Obedient, Radically Blessed, Leading Women to the Heart of God, Who Holds the Key to Your Heart?, Capture His Heart, Capture Her Heart, Living Life on Purpose, The Sweetest Story Ever Told* and co-author of *A Woman's Secret to a Balanced Life* with Sharon Jaynes. She is a featured writer for the *P31 Woman* monthly publication and has had her work published in other publications such as *Focus on the Family Magazine* and Larry Burkett's *Money Matters* newsletter.

Lysa has been featured numerous times on Dr. Dobson's Focus on the Family radio broadcast, as well as many other radio and television programs such as the "700 Club" and Moody's "Midday Connection." She was also the keynote speaker for Focus on the Family's "Renewing the Heart" women's leadership conference and is one of the featured Extraordinary Women speakers. She is a certified CLASS speaker and speaks from coast to coast at women's conferences, banquets and retreats. She and her husband Art also conduct marriage seminars for both men and women. Lysa and her family live just outside of Charlotte, North Carolina.

A Friend's Encouragement

Read Hebrews 13:1, 1 Samuel 14:7, Ecclesiastes 4:9-12, Proverbs 17:17, 1 Thessalonians 5:11

I have a friend who is a great encouragement to me. She cheers me on in my writing, prays for me, and never fails to listen when I have news or just need to talk. Because of her support, I know I have come further in my writing than I ever would have without her. Her wisdom and experience is invaluable and I feel blessed to have her to call on. I have heard it said that, while a close relationship with God is irreplaceable, sometimes a friend becomes "God with skin on." Since He can't physically be with me, He has sent her to serve in that capacity at times. She is God's gift to me for such a time as this.

This book came out of that relationship. I was struck one day by how blessed I am to have this person in my life. She had been so helpful to me as I got started in my publishing adventure. She freely gave me information and withheld nothing. She was not guarded or selfish with what she knew and always seemed to be thinking of me over herself. Not only did she encourage me that I was a good writer, she also believed in me enough to place her confidence in me—even at times when I had none! What's more, I just enjoyed having someone I could talk about writing with. One day she called me to share 1 Samuel 14:7 with me and I realized how rare it is to find a friend who is truly "with you, heart and soul."

As I thought of all of this, I began to pray and thank God for this person and her impact in my life. As I prayed, I told God that I knew her commitment to help me was rare—especially in a business as competitive as publishing. But knowing how much she had helped me made me realize what a priceless, selfless gift she had given me. That day, I promised God that if He ever gave me the opportunity to help someone else like she had helped me, I would. Perhaps I could make a positive difference in another writer's life. Perhaps my words of encouragement would be what God used to inspire another woman to write a book that would bless many others. I was excited at the prospect and thanked God in advance for this person He would someday bring into my life.

Over the next week, the idea and complete outline for this book came pouring out of me like a dam had burst. I had a sense of urgency that this book was the answer to my prayer. I was awed and humbled that God was entrusting me with this project. As I have watched this book take shape, I am amazed by the encouragement it will provide to those who read it. On a more grand scale than I could have imagined, this book is a way to touch the lives of those who read it the way my friend has touched mine.

God did not intend for us to go through life alone. He created the family and gave us friends so that we wouldn't have to. My prayer for this book is that, after having read it, you will feel that you have made a friend in me and in the other contributors who gave of their time and talents to make this book possible. Like me, these people all have a passion for helping other writers take those first tenuous steps towards fulfilling God's call on their lives. Take some time today to thank God for the path He has you on and the people you've met along the way. Celebrate His calling on your life, whatever it may be, and prayerfully commit to learn from this study and the wisdom and experience of these contributors.

Using the verses from today's reading, pick one or two and send them to a special friend in your life. A handwritten card is always a nice surprise, but an e-mail will do in a pinch. Take time today to be an encouragement to someone else!

The Power of Words

By: Linda Gilden

"You have nice handwriting."

That was my professor's comment on my college creative writing class essay—the essay that I was sure was a *Reader's Digest* shoo-in! I had worked hard and felt like I had done my very best in the class that would teach me how to achieve my dream of being a writer. I was crushed.

True, those are not negative words. But to an aspiring writer who longed to hear words of encouragement and praise, the comments on the paper might as well have said, "You'll never make it as a writer!"

The power of words. I realized in that one experience how powerful words can be if they are not chosen carefully. Even if I never published anything, I vowed to always choose my words carefully so they would have a positive influence in the lives of others. And, I put my writer's dream away.

Fifteen or so years later, after observing the amount of volunteer writing I was doing for my church and other organizations, my husband encouraged me to dust off my dream and attend a writer's conference. About the same time, my neighbor unexpectedly walked across the street and said, "I'm thinking about going to a writer's conference and I need a roommate! Want to go with me?"

Without a clue as to what a writer's conference was, I went. I was way out of my comfort zone but I soon knew I had discovered something really wonderful! There were many other people out there who also wanted to write to share God's message of love.

I shyly struggled through the first few days at the conference and then the thing I had feared most happened – an editor asked if he could talk to me. I knew he had read one of the manuscripts I had sent ahead to be critiqued. What should I say to him? Would I be rejected and discouraged again?

When we got together, he said, "You know what, I used to skip stones when I was a little boy!" (That was the subject of my article.) "I'd like to buy your article for my magazine."

I learned another wonderful thing – editors are kind and encouraging people with whom I can talk about my children. They are real, approachable people and we need to connect with their hearts! Good writing is not the only thing they look for.

After returning home, I scoured bookstores, libraries, and college catalogues to find out how I could learn more about being a writer. The dream I had squelched for so long had resurfaced with a new enthusiasm. The editor at that writer's conference had renewed that spark.

It was difficult to find instructional materials on writing for the Christian market. But I searched everywhere and sought out people who were already doing what I wanted to do. I also continued to attend conferences. And I began submitting articles to publications on a regular basis.

Several years later I began writing books. And who was one of the people I received congratulations from when my first book came out? The editor at the first writers' conference who bought my article about skipping stones!

When an opportunity came to teach at a national writer's conference, I was a little overwhelmed. But I realized God was opening big doors for me and I must obediently go through them.

Standing in front of "my" class, I was focused and excited to be sharing my writing journey with new writers and helping them discover the joy of being "print missionaries."

It was rewarding to feel that I was able to save them many steps along the way to being a writer because I could pass on what I had learned.

The more success I had in publishing books and articles, the more I realized how important it was to mentor other aspiring writers who are trying to find their way. As my list of writing credits grew and others noticed my bylines, people began to say to me, "I've always wanted to write. Can you help me?"

God not only called me to be a writer; He called me to help others be writers. My desire to educate myself in this field has led me to help educate, enable, and equip others.

I have found tremendous freedom in discovering the path God has created for me. It gives me the liberty to share freely with others without thought of competing with them. I know that God is my "agent" and has plenty of assignments for me. I rejoice in the success of others. The place that I occupy in the writing world is just for me!

My own writing ministry is multiplied by the writing successes of those I have helped learn to write. I will never truly know the scope of my writing ministry until I get to Heaven. The success of those I mentor is an extension of my own ministry. Every time someone reads an article or book written by someone I have mentored, I have a part in their success. Investing in the lives of other writers has an impact on many, many people.

Eric Liddell spoke to his sister in the movie *Chariots of Fire*. He addressed her concern about the Olympics interfering with his missionary career in China. "When I run," he said, "I feel God's pleasure."

I may not run but I have discovered that when I write, I feel God's pleasure.

This is not the end of my journey. In some ways it is just the beginning. As more books are added to my list of credits, I find I am doing more speaking. Again, God has directed me out of my comfort zone to a place where I must rely more heavily on Him. And I am finding His pleasure in sharing His message verbally.

Recently someone at church came up to me and said, "My husband saw your latest book sitting on the bedside table. He picked it up and started reading it. When he turned it over to read the bio, he said, 'Honey, did you know this author lives in the same town we do?' He was amazed." And I am as amazed as anyone at the doors God has opened for this shy Southern Belle!

As I continue to travel this God-directed journey, I can't wait to see where it will take me next. And I daily remind myself that it is not always the written, or even the spoken, word that makes the lasting impression.

"You show that you are a letter from Christ . . . written not with ink but with the Spirit of the living God, not on tablets of stone but on tablets of human hearts."
—2 Corinthians 3:3

I still have nice handwriting. But more than ever, I realize that what is written on paper is not the only thing that matters.

Linda Gilden is a wife, mother, speaker and author of *Love Notes in Lunchboxes,* released by New Hope Publishers. To learn more about Linda's speaking and writing, visit *www.lindagilden.com.*

The Love of Words

Read Psalm 33:6, John 1:14

If you are a writer, then chances are you have a love of words. You like to string them together in unusual ways, paint pictures with them and just play with them. Words are your tools. They work for you (most of the time), helping you communicate the message God has placed on your heart.

God loves words too. As the Creator, He could have shaped the universe with His hands or painted it into existence with a God-sized brush. But He didn't. In Genesis, we see the same phrase at each stage of creation: "God said." He literally spoke the world into being, using the power of words for the first time.

John 1:1 tells us that "In the beginning was the Word, and the Word was with God and the Word was God." The use of "word" in the Greek is "logos," which means word, thought or concept. Jesus was God's expression of Himself to us. Jesus had been with God at the time of creation and will be with God for eternity. Jesus Christ was God putting His words into action.

All throughout scripture, we see the significance of words. The Ten Commandments were words carved in stone. The Israelites were told, "Fix these words of mine on your hearts and minds; tie them as symbols on your hands and bind them on your foreheads. Teach them to your children" (Deuteronomy 11:18-19). The Bible says not to break our word (Numbers 30:2), to live according to the word (Psalm 119:9), to hide the word in our hearts (Psalm 119:11), to speak kind words (Proverbs 12:25), and to spread the word of the gospel (Matthew 28:18-20).

Most of all we are reminded of the power of the Word. Hebrews 4:12 tells us, "For the Word of God is living and active and sharper than any two-edged sword, it penetrates even to dividing soul and spirit, joints and marrow; it judges the thoughts and attitudes of the heart." James 1:22 goes a bit further in challenging us, "Do not merely listen to the Word, and so deceive yourselves. Do what it says."

God put His words into action by creating the world and then sending His son into that world. How can we as His servants and lovers of the Word take action and honor Him?

Using your Bible concordance, look up "word" and "speech." Write down any verses that particularly minister to you.

A Love Affair

. . . .

By: Rebecca Barlow Jordan

It started out as an innocent attraction. But as the years passed, it turned into a full-fledged love affair.

I can't remember exactly when I first fell in love with words. But as a child and teen, summer after summer I sat enthralled in my fantasy world—and read tales born out of the lives of ordinary characters, with consonants and vowels woven skillfully together through pluck and persistence. By whom? Writers. Writers opened to me worlds of mystery, romance, inspiration, poetry, fiction, and biographies. I loved them all. Each written page was a work of art, a sculpture of experiences, and of truthful lessons. Each book was a creative treasure of someone's imagination or divine inspiration.

Perhaps it happened that day in Mrs. Riley's 8th grade English class. It was one of those *ta-da-ta-da-ta-da-ta-da* rhymes penned by the idealistic fingers of a too-tall girl with her too-small God. "God's beauty lies around us . . . there's beauty everywhere." My very first poem—published in the National High School Poetry Association!

I didn't know it then, but the words of that poem would change my life forever. What did a homely, freckled-faced adolescent know about beauty? Yet I relished the honor of that first publication like a wide-eyed child ablaze with the wonder of Christmas.

Sadly, I soon forgot and packed away the beauty of that moment without realizing its significance—and without heeding the soft whisper between the lines: "Add beauty to my world."

Years later, I heard the whisper again as a young wife and mother, and it stirred something inside—something indefinable, an unfulfilled longing for something lofty and grand. I marveled at the musician, whose fingers danced on the ivories with sheer beauty, creating a symphony in the hearts of its listeners. But I shamed myself for chaining my heart to a pen and a desk, pouring out songs no one would ever hear—while dirty dishes and unfolded laundry sat untended. At times the whisper grew so loud I felt I could dance all night to the beat of my foolish heart. Then I would sigh and agree, "No beauty here," and I'd pack away my dancing shoes for a while.

I praised the teachers of my children, the silent heroes of education who could shape a mind and mold a heart for good. Oh, the beauty of knowing you had touched a thousand little lives, enriched a nation, and even changed the course of history because of your powerful influence.

Inventors and scientists and scores of influential people paraded through books and newspapers, taunting me—skilled artists whose contributions and whose lives would literally make a world of difference. But what about me? Did my dreams matter? How could I "add beauty to my world?" How could I make a difference?

Still I heard it—that unquenchable, divine voice from my childhood. I didn't know how to answer it. Yet I couldn't quiet it. I only knew the desire was growing—slowly, quietly—this longing to satisfy my Creator by somehow bringing beauty into my world. I prayed. I watched. I hoped. And finally I decided to try.

I started with greeting cards. When others asked about my work, sometimes I'd reply, "I'm a 'Band-Aid' dispenser"— because like band-aids, greeting cards temporarily comfort the hurts with laughter or consolation until permanent healing occurs and beauty is restored.

The words flew off my pen like they'd just been set loose from a prison of pent-up emotions. And editors actually bought my verses! So I decided to take a step further. I took a writer's correspondence course, then attended a series of writer's conferences. Fueled by a passion I could not explain, I kept writing, treasuring the sales and ignoring the rejections. At one conference, I won the "Persistence Award," with over 1000 rejections in that year. Years later, I taught at that same conference.

When editors asked, "Would you be willing to try something new?" each time I gulped and said, "Sure." Afterwards I'd moan to myself, "I've never done this before—I can't do it!" And then God would gently remind me that He would do it through me. Early on, I wrote more for myself, for the sheer beauty and enjoyment of painting pictures with words—rather than for the Artist Himself.

Life happened. Years passed. Times of confusion turned me aside for a while, but eventually I returned full circle to my first adolescent questions. How could I write about beauty when I couldn't even define it or find it? Could anyone, really? The words of George Eliot haunted me, "It's never too late to become the person you might have been."

I'm now older and hopefully wiser, and as I look back over my life, I see it all more clearly. I discovered beauty in the most unlikely places. Following a well-known, yet divine map, I began to uncover pieces of beauty—like buried treasure. I found beauty in the gentle and steadfast heart of a man in whom I could trust implicitly. It hovered in a simple kitchen, where even burnt, pitiful offerings turned to grateful, plentiful feasts. I discovered it in the soft lullabies of a too-young mom caressing her infant in the predawn hours, and in the arms of God-given passion, sustained now for almost four decades.

I listened to its voice beside Colorado rivers, and stood agape in its awesome presence surrounding snow-capped mountains. I watched it bloom in the moist earth of my backyard perennial garden, and felt its velvet coat on the petals of every dew-dropped rose. It welled up in my heart each time I introduced others to His Words, and to the joys of knowing my Creator for themselves. I embraced its truths and cried its tears as I watched my children pass through my life like sifted flour.

Beauty was all a part of a grand scheme—grander than my heart could ever dream or imagine. In reality, instead of discovering beauty, I think beauty found me. Like a grand orchestra leader my Creator had been conducting the symphony of my life all along. Whether anyone heard it or not, it was a song He gave me that would not end, the inspiration to keep adding something beautiful, even if it were only for the ears of my Creator Lover.

In time, the whisper grew louder and added a phrase: "Add My beauty . . . Write My words." And then it made sense. No fiery tongs from an angel's hand. No burning bush upon the mountainside. No blinding light from the sky. Just three words.

My words would probably never change a heart or move a nation—but His Words could. God's words, dressed in Heaven's clothing, could leap over walls of hatred, prejudice, ugliness, and despair. His Words, wrapped around the microphone of my pen could comfort, teach, love, and inspire others to be and do greater things than I could ever imagine.

Somewhere in the process, I learned to say "Yes," when my "divine Editor" asked me to do more. I began speaking His words to others who needed beauty and encouragement in conferences and various events. When I said, "I can't do this," God would simply smile and say, "That's all right. I can."

I'm still in a love affair, but not with words. Now when I hear His gentle whisper, "Add my beauty, write My words," I don't hesitate. Since I truly fell in love with the One who gives the words, I can honestly say, I no longer write for me. Now I write for Him.

And there's a fringe benefit: Sometimes using this gift of words is so much fun, I almost feel guilty getting paid for it.

But don't tell that to my editors.

Favorite writing quote:

"To love what you do and feel that it matters, how could anything be more fun?"
—*Author Unknown*

Favorite Bible verse:

"Faithful is He who called you, and He will also do it."

—*1 Thessalonians 5:24*

A best-selling inspirational author and speaker, **Rebecca Barlow Jordan** has authored numerous books, including the popular devotionals, *Daily in Your Presence and Daily in Your Image,* and *Courage for the Chicken Hearted* series—and over 1600 inspirational pieces such as greeting cards, articles, and gift products. She lives with her minister husband in Greenville, Texas.

Prepared To Share

Read I Peter 3:15, Colossians 4:6

If you are reading this book, then you probably have the same desire that Peter and Paul expressed in these verses. You have a story you long to tell others so that you can share how God has worked in your life.

There are several guidelines these verses provide for us all to remember:

1. **"Always be prepared."** But are we always prepared? It's one thing to be prepared to speak in front of hundreds of people, but it's another thing entirely to be prepared in the grocery store after a long day of dealing with kids, jobs, etc.
2. **"Do this with gentleness and respect."** People won't care how much you know until they know how much you care, as the saying goes. We must respect those we are reaching out to and not talk down to them. I'm sure most of us can remember a day when we were the one in the pew fumbling through the Bible to find the passage. I know I can!
3. **"Let your conversation be seasoned with salt, so that you may know how to answer everyone."** Just like salt keeps things from spoiling, so should we watch our words so that they will never be spoiled or corrupted. In these verses, the word "everyone" references all the people we come in contact with that do not know Jesus Christ.

Write down the three points we learned from these verses and how you can implement them in your daily life. Write down specific examples and commit to do these things.

From Darkness to Dreams

By: Mary Southerland

Dreams are the "stuff" of which a purpose-driven life is made. For many years, I dreamed of speaking to women across the world, sharing God's message of hope and restoration. God repeatedly arranged the circumstances of my life to confirm and fuel that dream. Therefore, I was not terribly surprised when God clearly carved out that path in my life, opening doors that only He could open. Each time I boarded an airplane, booked a speaking engagement or stood to share my story, I celebrated God's plan for this unlikely servant.

I loved teaching, but the thought of becoming a writer made my palms sweat, my heart beat faster and my stubborn will sit up and take notice. In fact, the idea of streaming words together in thoughts and sentences in order to create a literary work that could be understood or possess any amount of worth seemed more like a nightmare than a dream. While speaking and teaching came naturally, writing was more like the hard work of giving birth. God had a plan.

While sitting at the bottom of a deep, dark pit called "clinical depression", the Father lovingly, gently urged me into the habit of journaling my thoughts and emotions. What had once seemed painful became pleasurable, restorative instead of depleting. I had no energy to speak the words. I could only write them. It was in that two-year battle with darkness that God birthed a new dream—the dream to write.

Desperate for help in my battle with the darkness, I called or visited every bookstore in town, searching for someone who understood my pain, someone who had walked in my steps. The overwhelming majority of books I found were either so complex that I couldn't understand them or so shallow that they were worthless. Was I alone? Did no one understand my pain? Then I knew. I was in that pit of darkness for many reasons, but one of the main reasons was that God was giving me a new dream, a new vision, smack dab in the middle of incredible darkness, pain and emptiness. I had to tell my story so that others would know—there is hope for every dark moment of life and freedom from every pit. I had no idea how or where to start. Once again, I waited.

We misunderstand and wrestle with the purpose and power of God's waiting rooms, thinking that time spent waiting is wasted time. Waiting is neither passive nor wasteful. It is, however, active and productive, a God-ordained time of holy preparation. It is amazing to me that it was in the most broken time of my life that He gave me a new dream, the next chapter of life. Isaiah 45:3 explains, "I will give you the treasures of darkness, riches stored in secret places, so that you may know that I am the LORD, the God of Israel, who summons you by name." God has gone before us and, in every trial or difficult experience, has buried a treasure and stored a rich, secret reward. The only way we can uncover that treasure or obtain the reward is to walk through the darkness. Some lessons cannot be learned in the light and must be discovered in the darkness. One of the most valuable gifts of my experience in the pit was the amazing truth that God had called me to write.

While sitting at the bottom of that pit, unable to escape and at times, not sure I even wanted to escape the familiar darkness, the first whisperings of "Mary, tell your story" brushed across my soul. Again, I waited, pouring out my pain and fear in written words. As I waited, God redefined who I was, stripping away anything that would hinder His plan in my life until, finally, the darkness lifted and I stepped into the light of His healing. I just knew that if I could sit down at a computer, the book would write itself. I tried. It didn't. As I sought God, I had the sense that my healing was not complete. The written word is powerful and must be penned from a broken life that has been restored by God.

Once again, I waited. Two years later, I found myself on an airplane, headed to the guesthouse of a friend who lived in North Carolina. The time had come to write the book. For seven days and nights, I sat at my computer, watching the words rapidly appear on the screen before me. It was as if the book was writing itself. I couldn't type fast enough. The thoughts and memories tumbled over each other, spilling out of my soul onto the page and into the hands of God as an offering of praise. When the last word was written, I sat back in awe, praising God that He always empowers us to do what He calls us to do. *Coming Out of the Dark* was written and published. And oh, the lessons I learned!

Write your story. Everything that touches your life passes through God's hands, with His permission and for a reason. Writing is simply the record of God at work in your life, shared through your eyes and with your heart. Don't try to write someone else's story. It will lack integrity and authenticity. Write what you know and what you have experienced. God has entrusted you with a special message to share. Write it!

Be disciplined. Writing demands a delicate balance between inspiration and hard work. Sometimes, the words flow freely while, at other times, writing is simply a discipline. Set aside blocks of time each week for writing. When the words won't come, spend that time seeking God, consecrating it as an offering to the Giver of your gift, knowing it is His to do with as He pleases. One of my husband's closest friends is a well-known author who, when he first began writing, struggled with finding time to write. Dan encouraged him to set aside every Friday morning to write and then held him accountable to his commitment. Bob Barnes has now written and published over ten books. God always honors discipline.

Walk away. When the creative juices stop flowing, stop writing. Walking away for even a few minutes will many times bring fresh perspective. The best way to rest from mental activity is to engage in physical activity. While writing a bible lesson, I hit a wall. Words and thoughts would not come. My husband and children were playing basketball, so I joined them for a quick game of "Horse". When I came back to my computer, I finished the lesson in a matter of minutes.

Never give up. Many writers are discouraged to the point of giving up when their manuscript is rejected. Because God always provides where He guides, know that your Father will bring the right publisher for your book. All publishers make mistakes. While speaking for a pastor's wives conference in California, I met the senior acquisition editor of a large publishing company. I took the opportunity to quiz him on what to do when a manuscript is rejected. "That is only one publisher's opinion," he said. With a sheepish smile, he then explained, "Mary, our publishing company turned down Veggie Tales." Never give up!

Keep writing. Make writing a daily habit in your life. Writing is like a muscle. The more you use it the stronger it will become.

Today, it is hard to say which I love most—speaking or writing. It seems that I love speaking the most, when I am speaking, and writing the most, when I am writing. Either way, I am living God's dream for my life.

Mary Southerland is a pastor's wife, mother of two and founder of Journey Ministry, a speaking and writing ministry dedicated to equipping every woman for her life journey. Mary's passion is to encourage women to be all that they can be in Jesus Christ! Through humor, transparency and solid biblical teaching, Mary leads women to discover the powerful and practical truth of God's word. Mary has a deep burden for women in ministry and is a frequent speaker for Pastor's Wives retreats and conferences. While she has developed resources addressing the unique needs of the pastor's wife and women in ministry, her message is for all women everywhere!

A dynamic teacher, Mary delivers a powerful message that strengthens the heart. She will make you laugh, cry and walk away thirsting for more of God.

Mary has spoken to thousands of women all over the United States, as well as in Latin America, South Africa, New Zealand, Costa Rica and the United Kingdom. Mary has an extensive tape ministry that speaks to the heart of women in every season of life. Mary and her family live in Waxhaw, NC. She is the author of *Coming Out of the Dark,* a book that chronicles her journey from the darkness of clinical depression to a life filled with light and hope. Mary's second book, *Sandpaper People* will be released July 1, 2005 by Harvest House Publishers. For more information, visit Mary's web page at *www.marysoutherland.com.*

Turning Back

Read Luke 22:32

When we go through hard times in our lives, it is tempting to wonder if anything good could possibly come from our trials. Our suffering and waiting seems endless and then, the clouds clear and a blue sky emerges. As we take inventory of our lives, we can see the reasons and answers begin to emerge. We stand amazed at Our Creator's ability to truly make "beauty from ashes" (Isaiah 61:3). So what is our next step after the trouble has passed?

The answer to that lies in today's passage. Jesus says to Peter, "I have prayed for you that your faith may not fail." As we are facing life's hardships, Jesus is there, cheering us on in the faith. What a beautiful image this brings to mind! Hebrews 12:1 tells us, "Therefore, since we are surrounded by such a great cloud of witnesses, let us throw off everything that hinders and the sin that entangles, and let us run with perseverance the race marked out for us." Hebrews 7:25 says that Jesus, "lives to intercede for us," just as He did for Peter. I get so excited when I think about the heroes of the faith, led by Jesus, praying for our success!

The next part is up to us. After the clouds clear and we have withstood the storm, we must "turn back and strengthen our brothers." I picture a soldier in a bloody battle. He fights his way out of the jungle, away from the gunfire and danger, to a place of refuge. As he pauses to catch his breath, he looks around to discover his buddy is not with him. There is no time to sit and decide what to do, no precious moments allowed to count the cost. He does the only thing he can. He turns around and goes back in after his friend.

Have you faced something big, scary and terrible in your life? Is God calling you to go back in and rescue a sister who is crying out, "Help me!" Make no mistake, this is a battle we are in. May we turn back to strengthen our sisters by telling our stories of God's faithfulness.

What is your story? Write down your five-minute testimony. Very briefly tell where you were before you met Christ, what happened when you met Christ, and where you are today because of your relationship with Him. Look for opportunities to share your story, asking God to show you specific people that need to hear from you.

One Author's Journey

By: Elise Arndt

Our life is like a book, filled with amazing stories that, when shared, God can use to change a life. From 1967–1972, in my life, preparation was taking place. God was writing His book in my heart that eventually would be a published work.

Living among a primitive tribal people in Papua New Guinea, I received an education during those years that textbooks could not provide. Experiences shaped my life, placing within me the desire to share with others the marvelous workings of God.

I wanted to write but the only way I knew how to do it was by putting my thoughts into letters. Isolated from people of my own culture, these letters were often used as a coping mechanism to deal with loneliness.

Words flowed from my heart in a free and uninhibited fashion. These letters expressed to friends and family my life as a missionary. I found I had an audience. The more they responded the more I wrote. The more I wrote the more my confidence grew.

When the thought entered my mind of serious writing I struggled with my ability. How could the technique of letter writing transfer into the enormous task of writing a book? Would anyone be interested? What about my credentials? How would I begin? In the midst of the turmoil came the promise of Ephesians 3:20. "Now to him who is able to do immeasurably more that all we ask or imagine according to his power that is at work within us."

Upon returning to the United States in 1973, I was humbled by God's promised provision as the process began. Over the course of many years I shared my stories with anyone who would listen. Eventually groups of women asked me to speak at Bible studies and conferences. Out of necessity, outlines developed which later were used as the basis for writing two books.

In 1980 I met a wonderful Christian author by the name of Daisy Hepburn. Our hearts immediately connected and I shared with her my passion for someday writing. Daisy's willingness to call her editor and give a recommendation amazed me. In the meantime she suggested I develop a proposal with an outline and several sample chapters.

The thought of preparing a proposal automatically produced the fear of rejection. My husband sensed my anxiety and gave me one of his infamous "sermons". "Elise, you are 37 years old. Take the risk! Begin writing! I don't want to hear you say at age 60, 'I wish I would have at least tried.' To live in regret is more painful and longer lasting than the rejection of a publisher. Getting published should not be your primary goal. Concentrate on leaving a legacy for our children. That alone will make it a success."

Soon after my discussion with Daisy I received a call from Carol Streeter of Victor Books (now Victor Chariot) wanting an interview. A proposal was submitted, accepted and a contract signed. Now came the disciplined process of serious writing.

The easiest part of writing is talking about doing it "someday". The hardest part is actually doing it by taking action, sitting in front of a computer and beginning the task. For me the pain of not writing exceeded the pain of writing. To do it meant sacrifice. To not do it meant regret. Despite what I knew was ahead, I consciously submitted to begin the process.

Words did not come easy. Since I am not a linear thinker, I used the process of brainstorming. Sentence structure, punctuation and capitalization were put aside as I concentrated on concepts, and creative ideas. The organization of these thoughts would come later.

Eventually a first draft developed which appeared great until I read it the next day. If this happens to you, don't be surprised. Have patience. Re-writes are part of the life of the writer. Each re-write makes you a better writer, causing you to evaluate the use of your words and the clarity of presenting your thoughts.

My perception when chapters were completed and submitted was this: "Hurray! Let's celebrate! My part is finished!" My editor's reaction was "They need more work—RE-WRITE". I responded "not again" as chapters came back marked with red pencil. I wanted to get the job done quickly. She strived for excellence. Frustration grew. This is where communication between author and editor is critical. And this is where tenacity and discipline play their biggest part.

In March of 1983, God's provision materialized. *A Mother's Touch* was published. In August of 1987 *A Mother's Time* followed. The hours I labored, the sacrifice of time that could have been spent with friends and family, the late nights and early mornings trying to meet deadlines, all seemed worth it as I gazed upon this finished work. In my hands was not just a published book but also a legacy—a treasure, a miracle of God's grace that would be passed on to future generations.

As a first time writer you enter the realm of the unknown. Writing is tedious and sometimes monotonous work. It is a craft that needs to be practiced daily just as singing, or playing an instrument. The more you write the better writer you become.

Good writers also read good authors; not just "how to write books." Fiction and non-fiction, Christian and secular works become a classroom in the school of writing. By reading and studying great authors you learn how to use words and transition thoughts.

Good writers educate themselves. They attend writer's conferences. Meet with editors. Talk with other authors. They take the risk of having their writing critiqued and look at the red pencil marks as a way of improving their writing.

Good writers know that re-writes are a fundamental part of writing. Even skilled writers have crummy first drafts. Adequately expressing the sacred thoughts of one's soul in words cannot be hurried. It takes time to write a good piece. Although tedious, these re-writes produce clarity to the reader, revealing more and more of the writer's heart.

Writing brings you into the world of emotional highs and lows. Discouragement and confidence walk side by side. As you journey, do not forget that the time you spend writing is never wasted time. Through your diligence comes the possibility of planting seeds of God's love and faithfulness in the hearts and minds of future generations. This reality alone can bring joy into the hours spent in front of your computer.

Embrace this new experience. Take the risk, even though fear of failure looms in the shadows. Write for the pure joy of expressing your heart on paper. By doing so you open yourself to live in a world free of regret. A world that might pleasantly surprise you with the "immeasurably more" promised in Ephesians 3:20.

Elise Arndt, author of *A Mother's Touch* and *A Mother's Time*, is an active Bible teacher, and conference speaker. She is the mother of five children and grandmother to ten. Before settling in Troy, MI Elise and her pastor husband served as missionaries to Papua New Guinea.

Desert Times

Read Exodus 2:15-22, Isaiah 30:21-22

When I graduated from college with a writing degree, I decided I should write a book. Since I had a new baby, I decided that it would be fitting to write a book on motherhood. As I planned my literary debut, it never occurred to me that perhaps I should be a little more experienced in my chosen field before I attempted to write about it!

Slowly but surely, God revealed to me that I was not ready to tackle the subject of motherhood, and He closed the doors on my writing pursuits one by one. Rather grudgingly, I settled into the life of a stay-at-home mom. I came to resent this calling on my life as I longed to see my name in print and fulfill what I was convinced was God's plan for me. Oh, how much I had to learn!

What I did not realize at that time was that those years where I felt frozen and stagnant were actually an essential part of God's plan for me. God allowed me to go through a time of preparation so that I would be equipped to reach others. Through the years of raising small children, dealing with a child's serious illness, building a marriage, and growing in Christ, I began to file away significant life lessons to share with others. My story began to take shape through this time of preparation. Just as God used Moses' time in the desert to prepare him, God allowed me to go through a desert time of my own. As I emerged from my desert time, I realized that God had done a remarkable work in me. He had taken all the bitterness and resentment in my life and replaced it with peace and contentment. I no longer yearned to see my name in print, but was happy just to write my story across my children's hearts. It was then that God whispered, "Now I can use you."

My idols of publishing and achievements had truly been forgotten as I sought out God's plan for my life, and walked in His ways. I cast my selfish pursuits aside as useless and He became the true desire of my heart.

Do you have dreams that have become barriers to your relationship with the Lord? Pray that God would reveal to you any area in your life that you have put ahead of Him. Ask Him to help you cast those aside and say, "Away with you."

My Daring Adventure

By: Mary DeMuth

"All writing comes by the grace of God."
—Ralph Waldo Emerson

I've wanted to be a writer since my second grade teacher praised my creativity. Something about how she said it made me wonder if the gift I'd seen in my father would be passed down to me in some sort of mystical impartation.

I scribbled adolescent angst into my diary, wondering in pen if life had purpose, if my small world meant something. It wasn't until fifteen when I heard about Jesus Christ and His outrageous death on a cross that I understood my life had rhyme *and* reason. At that moment, I experienced the truth of this verse: "But God has chosen the foolish things of the world to shame the wise, and God has chosen the weak things of this world to shame the things which are strong" (1 Corinthians 1:27). I pictured myself, messy and forlorn, being rescued by God. "I want that one," He said. "The weak and foolish one. I'm going to declare Myself through her."

So, I wrote. And wrote some more. I typed my way through an English major, met a Jesus-loving man, got married and started a family. When my daughter Sophie was still an infant, the need to put finger to keyboard surfaced. After reading several newsletters and books about thrift—we had little money back then—I realized that they lacked an important element. Their steps to thrift nirvana were paved with the goal of saving at any cost. I wanted to provide people with a different perspective: that we save in order to give. *The Giving Home Journal,* a subscriber-based newsletter, was born.

I published the newsletter three years until my second child cried his way into the world. Between baby boy two and baby girl three, I wrote curriculum, ad copy and edited church newsletters. I made myself have deadlines. I continued to write in my "diary," which had now been more appropriately named "journal." I started writing short stories and Bible studies. I wrote query letters that elicited rejections.

But it wasn't until my youngest daughter started attending preschool that I gave full attention to my dream of becoming a writer. I'd been in the process of becoming one for a decade, laboring in obscurity.

On my first day of attending a new church, I met a real writer—one who had several published books and articles. She was the editor of an award-winning magazine, and for some amazing reason, we became friends. Sandi helped me craft a query letter from the pieces of my confused tries. Within a few months, I sold my first article to a well-known marriage magazine.

I decided that I wanted to be a newspaper columnist, so I researched our local paper, noting the lack of one, and sent several samples along with a query to its editor. We met in his musty-smelling office. "How about 25 dollars a column? It's not much, but it's something," he told me. I took it! For three years, I wrote a weekly lifestyle column for an audience of 100,000 Dallas-area residents.

Still, I had always wanted to write a novel. I had a file folder three inches thick full of research about a small town in Ohio during the Great Depression, how the rock quarry foreman (my great grandfather) was killed underneath a crumbling embankment. I had taped interviews where my great aunts and uncles recounted the tenacity of my great grandmother, how she did everything to hold her family of seven children together amid the backdrop of staggering poverty. I wanted to write her story, but I didn't know if I had it in me to create a convincing story arc.

About this time, I found a local Christian writer's group that met in a large church near my home. The first meeting I worried that my words would be annihilated or scorned. Instead, I met writers just like myself, wanting to be published, wanting to glorify Jesus in the process. This group of writers became some of my closest friends. Through their encouragement I started my novel. My new friend Leslie told me about the importance of writer's conferences. We attended a local one-day conference that year, and with her insistence, I registered for the 2003 Mount Hermon Christian Writer's Conference.

The looming conference gave me the boost I needed to write my novel. In less than six months, I completed it, readying it for editor's eyes. While at the conference, I attended an agent's morning track. He told us the first day of class that he wasn't taking any new authors, that his "stable was full." Still, we met, chatted, and talked about my manuscript. Three weeks after the conference, he emailed me, asking to represent me. When I screamed, my children thought I had injured myself! When I spilled the news to them and to my wondering husband, we danced in the computer room.

My first novel didn't sell to a publisher. Apparently Depression-era fiction is a tough sell. I wrote a second novel and it didn't sell either. After I had completed that novel, my agent emailed me and wrote, "Mary, you really ought to write a parenting book." Since my children were often the subjects of my weekly column, he felt like I had a knack for capturing family life.

My first reaction was *no way*. Like any parent, I felt inadequate, unable to impart any sort of parental wisdom. Still, he pestered me. Finally, I shot him an e-mail that said, "The only book I'd ever write about parenting would be for those of us who don't want to duplicate the homes we were raised in."

"Write that book," he wrote.

I had never written a proposal before. At this point, I was sure I'd be a fiction writer. A proposal seemed impossible, unreachable. I couldn't seem to wrap my mind around marketing, comparative analysis, or target audience. Thankfully, my friend Leslie loaned me several of her proposals. With those as examples, I completed the parenting proposal. Within a month, a major publishing house picked up *Pioneer Parenting* (to be published January 2006). I did another dance!

My agent also connected me to Hearts at Home who wanted to have a devotional for their conference attendees. I pulled together a proposal and they liked it. That book, *Ordinary Mom, Extraordinary God* (Harvest House) turned out to be my first release in February 2005.

Since then, I've started another novel, written a portion of a book about girls who gave everything to Jesus, and written two more non-fiction proposals. By God's grace, I'll be teaching a major morning track at Mount Hermon Christian Writer's Conference with my agent.

It's amazing to me what has happened in just two years. My dream to be a full-time writer is coming to fruition, not merely because of my tenacity to put words to page, but because God has graced my writer's journey with amazing people who stopped to help me. I can trace His nuances on my path, how He enabled me to labor in obscurity, encouraged me through rejection, and invigorated my life in such a way that I actually *had* something to write about.

Helen Keller states, "Life is either a daring adventure or nothing." It's been difficult being a writer. Facing constant rejection and angry, blank screens is trying. But, I'd rather take the risk on the daring adventure God has for me than tuck my dream away in a diary, never to see the light of day.

Mary DeMuth was a columnist for Star Community Newspapers in Dallas and has appeared in several well-known Christian magazines. Her debut book, *Ordinary Mom, Extraordinary God*, released February 2005. DeMuth, a thirty-eight-year-old stay-at-home mother of Sophie, Aidan and Julia and the wife of a church planter, lives in Southern France.

Stepping Out of The Desert

Read Exodus 3:11, Exodus 4:1-2

When God called me to step out and begin writing and speaking, I was in a comfortable place in my life. I had learned to love the desert and had pitched my tent there to stay. I had become so accepting of where God had me that I had no desire to step out of my comfort zone. I kept thinking I would write *someday*—and it felt safe to just defer my dreams indefinitely. At least then I did not have to take risks.

But God was having none of that. Through my Bible study, specific experiences and some trusted counsel, He began to impress upon me that it was time to begin writing, and worse, speaking. I was fearful—of failing, of disappointing my family, of letting God down. I questioned my ability, my preparation, my worth. The once-cocky college grad had become a cautious, doubtful woman.

When God encountered Moses in the desert, he was pretty comfortable himself. He had a wife, children and a life. He wanted nothing more than to stay right where he was, just like me. His palace life in Egypt was long forgotten, his kingly aspirations left behind—and that was okay by him. He saw no need to do more, and even doubted his usefulness when God did call him. What he did not realize was that God had taken all of his life experiences—from the river to the palace to the desert—and pronounced Moses ready to serve. He needed nothing more than what he held in his hand, and a willing heart. God's work in him was by no means complete—it never would be. And yet, it was time for him to leave his comfort zone and go where God commanded.

We all know the rest of Moses' story. God took just what he held in his hand and used it to accomplish His purposes for His people. What is the rest of your story? What is it you hold in your hand? A pen? A computer mouse? A microphone? Whatever it is, I can guarantee that God will use it for His glory if you willingly offer it up to Him.

Write down three life experiences God has allowed you to have so that you will be prepared to serve Him. Pray over these three experiences and offer them up to Him, thanking Him for placing these things in your hand.

Confirming God's Call to Write

By: Glynnis Whitwer

What does a "real" writer look like? I've asked myself that question at least a hundred times. The reason? I don't think I look like a "real" writer.

When I think of a writer, I imagine someone who has loved to write stories since they were a little child. Their imaginative mind must have overflowed with characters, descriptive phrases, intricate plots and creative dialog.

They probably kept a diary and secreted away to write for hours—pouring their heart and soul into words, and dotting their "i's" with hearts.

A "real" writer certainly feels a compulsion to write at all times. If they didn't write, they would surely fade away and become a dusty pile of nothing. Writing, for a "real" writer, brings them life. Right?

Well, I don't fit that description. I've never imagined stories, much to my children's dismay. I might come up with an interesting character, but their story is boring even to my ears. I've never once written in a diary. Even as a young girl, I was always afraid someone would find it and read my innermost thoughts. And I don't think I'll wither away if I don't write.

How can God call someone like me to write, when I don't think I have the characteristics of a writer? Over the years, I've come to realize that writing is just a part of what God has called me to do, which is teach. For me, writing is a means to an end—communicating God's truth to fellow travelers on this road of life. To do that, God has called me to write.

My story starts as a young girl with a dream to be a teacher. My Dad was a high school teacher and when I was old enough to use an answer key, I would help him grade multiple-choice tests. I loved stacking the test papers in a neat pile, using a red pen and figuring out the percentage grade. Maybe it's part of why I love office product stores. Aisles of pens, notepads and binders can set my heart racing.

That dream to teach continued through grade school, but was lost somewhere in high school. I think I'd heard enough of my Dad's frustration with the "administration" for teaching to lose its golden glow. Reality set in, and teaching didn't have the same appeal once I understood its cost.

After two years in college I still didn't know what I wanted to be when I grew up. It wasn't until I happened upon a brochure promoting public relations as a career. I remember reading through the qualifications and I fit every one: good writer, likes people, likes organizing special events and passionate about communicating a message. Two and a half years later, I graduated from Arizona State University with a degree in journalism and public relations. (ASU didn't have a pure Public Relations degree).

I started working in the field and loved it. I loved writing other people's stories, business articles, brochures and ad copy. But I didn't like the promotion aspect of it all. I disliked talking to newspapers, television and magazine editors, trying to get them to cover my event or company. So, a few years into it, God resurfaced my dream to teach and I went back to school to get a teaching certificate.

After a few semesters, I changed jobs and found one that allowed me to write more than promote and I dropped the dream of teaching again.

Fast-forward 10 years. I had three boys and my family moved to Charlotte, North Carolina. It is clear in hindsight that God directed that move, because I connected with Proverbs 31 Ministries in a way that only God can orchestrate.

We had been church searching and God directed us to a small congregation meeting in a grade school. A few weeks later, a lovely young woman gave her testimony. My heart was moved by her honesty and obvious love for God. That very same week, I was driving and heard a radio spot by the woman who had spoken at church. God spoke to me in a way I'd never before experienced and He clearly told me to track her down and offer my services as a volunteer. It took a few phone calls, but I finally reached Lysa TerKeurst, the President of Proverbs 31 Ministries.

"Hi Lysa," I said. The next words came tumbling out of my mouth as I blurted, "I've just moved to Charlotte, I saw you at church, then heard you on the radio. I've got a degree in journalism and I'm wondering if you need any volunteers."

There was a pause on the other end of the phone before Lysa answered, "We've been praying for someone with a degree in journalism."

I met with Lysa and Sharon Jaynes, then Vice President of the ministry, and within a few weeks was selecting the best articles from the first seven years of the ministry and editing their second compilation book. The month I finished the book, their newsletter editor resigned, and I was offered that position. That was in 1999 and I've loved it ever since.

Writing before Proverbs 31 was a job. I never considered it a calling. People paid me to write flattering copy about a company, a product or professional people. It was easy to go to work, and write about someone else.

When I was led to Proverbs 31, I felt God calling me to write about something close to my heart, my intimate thoughts, my understanding of Him and His truths, my personal experiences. But I hesitated responding to that call. "That's what 'real' writers write about," I thought. "Not me – no one wants to hear my thoughts or experiences."

As I looked at other writers around me, I continued to doubt that call on my life. You see, I didn't have a collection of stories I'd written over the years like Sharon did. I didn't write just to write like Lysa did. I didn't **look** like the other writers I saw. Those writers were passionate about writing. I wasn't. While I loved to write, to me it was a job.

But God was gentle and persistent, and one day reminded me of my childhood dream to teach. God showed me that although I had neglected that dream at times throughout my life, He had never forgotten it. He invited me to consider that He could take my dream, reshape it, align it with His will and hand it back to me. Although it now looked different from my childhood dream, it was a fulfillment of His call on my life and a dream He had placed in my heart years ago.

God is now fulfilling my dream to teach through writing. And that makes me a writer. I will never have the characteristics of other writers, but God designed me differently. I do approach writing like a job, but that's okay. I'm still called by God to write, and teach.

Perhaps you feel unqualified to write. I know how that feels – even with a degree in writing, I still felt unqualified to write for years. But God can be trusted. If He has put a call on your life to write, then He has a purpose for your writing. You don't have to look like any other writer - in fact it's good if you don't. God has called you to write, because of who you are.

I encourage you to embrace your calling to write. Be who you are and don't compare yourself to anyone. In doing so, you will confirm God's call on your life and bring Him glory and honor.

Glynnis Whitwer has been married to Tod for 21 years and together they have three boys: Joshua, Dylan and Robbie. Glynnis is also the Editor of the P31 Woman Magazine, published by Proverbs 31 Ministries. She's contributing author to two books and has been published in national magazines. She's active in women's and children's ministry in her home church in Glendale, Arizona, and speaks to women's groups across the country. For information visit *www.proverbs31.org* and click on "Speaking Ministry."

No Excuses

Read Exodus 4:12

When God first called me out of my comfort zone of kids and carpools to write and to speak for Him, I had a whole list of reasons as to why I wasn't ready, or worthy. God removed my excuses one by one, and assured me that I was ready and worthy, simply because He said so. I thought I would list out the excuses I offered up to Him, and what He had to say about each one:

I said: "I'm not qualified."
God said: 2 Corinthians 12:9
I said: "I'm too busy."
God said: Matthew 6:33
I said: "I'm not prepared for this."
God said: Hebrews 13:20-21
I said: "But, I'm afraid."
God said: Joshua 1:9

Do any of these excuses sound familiar? As you can see, God's word shows us how absolutely senseless it is to stammer out our pitiful excuses in the face of God's calling. He will equip us. He will sustain us. He will make a way. And He will be glorified in the process.

What excuses are you offering up to God today? Write them down and then take a moment to pray over them. Don't let Satan bind you with those excuses any longer. Give them to God and let Him remove them. Replace your excuses with the Truth of His word.

How Did I Get to this Place?

By: Sharon Jaynes

I will never forget that day. I was sitting in a meeting at Moody Publishing, a division of Moody Bible Institute in Chicago, Illinois. Seated around the mahogany conference table were ten men and two women, all who were publishing professionals: the Vice President of Moody Publishing, Director of Marketing, Acquisitions Editor, International Marketing, and more. The men dressed in dark suits with patterned ties, sat angled with their heads turned toward one eastern North Carolina girl sharing her book proposals. I explained the purpose, passion, and proposed outline for Being a Great Mom, Raising Great Kids. They asked questions and I did my best to answer. Then we moved on to Celebrating a Christ Centered Christmas: Ideas from A-Z.

"I know you don't typically publish holiday books," I began.

"We do now," Bill excitedly interrupted with a twinkle in his eye.

About two hours into our meeting, one of the men leaned in and stopped me. "Sharon, do you mind me asking. . . . What was your major in college?"

"Dental Hygiene," I sheepishly replied. "I have a Bachelor of Science degree in Dental Hygiene."

A chuckle rolled around the room.

"I thought it was probably something totally unrelated," he concluded.

I never asked what he meant by that response. But my hope was that he suspected what God had just whispered in my ear.

See, while I was talking to the team, using track one of my mind, track two was talking to me. *How did you get to this place? Why do these important people look so interested in what you are saying? What are you doing here?* Then I heard God's still small voice . . . *I brought you here.*

And that, my friend, is my story. As you read biographical accounts of men and women with childhood dreams of one day becoming published authors, there is at least one who did not– me. I am embarrassed to even tell you this, but when I was growing up, I had very little interest in reading or writing. When my parents sold my childhood home, my husband, Steve, helped us clean out their attic. Among the dusty clutter was a box filled with faded Cliff Notes. For those more studious among us, Cliff Notes are the little books that summarize books on college and high school reading lists. They outline the plot, describe the main characters, and help those undisciplined or uninterested students pass tests in English class.

"My goodness," Steve exclaimed as he looked through my collection. "Did you ever actually read a book in high school?"

"I can't recall one," I teased.

After high school, I went off to college to major in dental hygiene. For four years I focused on science and math with a few liberal arts classes thrown in for fun. But something happened to me when my son, Steven, was born. God stirred in me a voracious appetite for books. I went back and acquired a high school reading list and read what I was supposed to have read years before. I went to the young reader section of the library and checked out book after book, discovering the treasures I had missed as a child. *Little Women, Jo's Boys, All Things Great and Small.* I grew to love Jane Eyre and her Mr. Rochester. I wept with Hester Prynne of the Scarlet Letter, and I laughed out loud at the exploits of Anne of Green Gables. As I began to delve into the wonderful storehouse of literature, God began to turn the knob to a hidden door of my life. Oh, it wasn't hidden to God, but simply unexplored by me. Just as a child who discovers a hidden door in a labyrinth of rooms of a sprawling mansion, God placed his hand on the handle of an unexplored chamber of my heart and soul. Then ever so slowly, the light from within peeked through the crack.

I began to see stories in my everyday life. God used nature, my child, other people, and circumstances to paint beautiful pictures to illustrate His character and His ways. Yet, instead of using paint and brush, God chose the medium of words. As my mind became alert to the life around me, I began to write down those stories. Never did I expect those first writings to be anything more than simple journal entries that those who would come behind me might enjoy.

So for ten years, I wrote modern day parables and kept them in a file in a drawer. Then one day, God decided to open yet another door – a passageway, really. Only this door did not lead to another hidden room. It led to the outside world and beyond. It was time to take the treasures God had shared with me and sprinkle them like ticker tape for anyone who would hear.

But I had a big hurdle to jump before I could actually walk through the threshold and out into the world. As a child, I was raised in a home filled with tension. It seemed as though our home was built on an emotional fault line and I never knew when "the big one" was going to hit. There were many big ones. I saw many things that a little child should never see and heard many things that a little child should never hear. I remember going to bed at night, pulling the covers tightly against my chin and praying that I could go to sleep to shut out the yelling and hitting going on in the next room.

My early years were wrapped in fear and feelings of inferiority, insecurity, and inadequacy. But when I was fourteen, I met Jesus Christ! The mother of one of my friends gently and persuasively loved me into a relationship with God that forever changed my life. However, I went from being an insecure non-Christian to an insecure Christian. I wish I could tell you that all those feelings of inadequacy melted away the moment I said yes to Christ, but they did not. I did not even realize that they were the chains that hung around my neck and drug behind my gait.

It was those insecurities that kept me from walking through the new passageway out into the world to share my writings. I had a glimpse of what could be, but I did not have the confidence to take the first step to get there. So I only looked at the door to the outside, but retreated to explore another area that needed to be uncovered first.

God took me on a journey to discover three simple truths: who I was in Christ, where I was in Christ, and what I had in Christ. I began to see that my perception of who I was and God's acknowledgement of who I was, were totally juxtaposed. He lovingly led me on a journey of discovering who I became the moment I accepted Christ . . . my new identity as a child of God. The space of this chapter does not allow for me to share all those truths with you; however, the journey of overcoming feelings of inferiority, insecurity, and inadequacy by understanding my new identity in Christ is the subject of my book, *Ultimate Makeover.* It was not my first book, but without the life transforming lessons found in *Ultimate Makeover,* there would have not been others.

Think back with me for a moment. The day before Jesus began His earthly ministry, He was baptized by His cousin John. When Jesus came up out of the water, God said, "You are my Son, whom I love; with you I am well pleased" (Luke 3:22 NIV). That is where God had to take me before I could begin this new journey of writing. First I had to hear God say . . . "You are my daughter whom I love; with you I am well pleased." He had said it in His Word, but I had never accepted it as truth.

And that, my friend, is where you must start as well.

Once I understood that I was not a pauper, but a child of the King, I had the confidence to go back to that open door leading to the passageway, walk across the threshold, and go out into the world. I took my writings and laid them at Jesus' feet. I didn't give them to God. I simply gave them back to God.

There are still days when I ponder . . . *how did I get to this place?* And God still echoes . . . *I brought you here.*

Sharon Jaynes is the Vice President of Proverbs 31 Radio, radio co-host, and international speaker. She is the author of nine books, including *Becoming a Woman to Who Listens to God*, *Becoming the Woman of His Dreams*, and *Ultimate Makeover*. Sharon has been featured on many TV and radio programs such as Family Life Today with Dennis Rainey and Aspiring Women. Her magazine articles have appeared in various magazines including Focus on the Family, Decision, and Crown Financial Concepts. She lives in Charlotte, North Carolina with her husband, Steve, and they have one grown son. Sharon can be reached at *sharonjaynes.com* or *sharon@proverbs31.org*.

Some Unlikely Heroes

Read Judges 3:9-31, Habakkuk 1:5

Are you making excuses as to why you aren't fit for Kingdom work? Today's verses give us a glimpse into the lives of three unlikely heroes—Othniel, Ehud and Shamgar. These men could have made excuses but chose to trust God instead.

Othniel relied on the Holy Spirit to accomplish within him what God had set out for him to do. He knew that he could not do what needed to be done in his own strength. Before Pentecost, people did not have the indwelling of the Holy Spirit like we have available to us through Christ (John 14:16-17). The Holy Spirit was only available at certain times for certain tasks. Judges 3:10 tells us that "the Spirit of the Lord came upon Othniel" and he was able to beat insurmountable odds as a result. Othniel is a great lesson to all of us on relying on the power of the Holy Spirit within us to accomplish what we may see as impossible. We are blessed to always have the Holy Spirit at work in us.

Ehud was disabled according to the standards of his time. He was left handed, and that was seen as a defect. Ehud could have pronounced himself useless, but he knew the truth: his success had nothing to do with his abilities or his weaknesses, and everything to do with allowing God to use him. Ehud knew the truth of Zechariah 4:6, "Not by might, nor by power, but by my Spirit, says the Lord Almighty."

Lastly, we arrive at Shamgar, "who struck down 600 Philistines with an oxgoad. He too saved Israel" (Judges 3:31). This verse does not seem so remarkable until you take into account that Israel had no weapons available to them at that time, as they were under severe oppression. Shamgar could have argued with God that he did not have any weapons, so how could he fight? Instead he used what he had on hand—an oxgoad, a blade normally used for cleaning a plow. And with that, he was able to do the impossible.

What excuses are you making today? Offer up what little you have and wait for the amazing things God will do!

Write down Habakkuk 1:5 and claim this verse for your own life. Thank God for giving us the example of Othniel, Ehud and Shamgar.

A Writing Life

An Interview with Carla Williams

Life has provided Carla Williams with plenty of material. In addition to being a pastor's wife and mother of three sons, she has also opened her home to twenty-eight young people and forty adults. Throughout thirty years of marriage, college students, confused teens, battered wives, and newly released prisoners have all found a place of refuge in the Williams' home. "It's been an interesting lifestyle that God has called us to," she chuckles. "And my writing definitely comes from that."

Carla began writing as a young woman through ministry opportunities like re-writing curriculum for children's ministry and writing and leading women's Bible studies. Over time, she developed a manuscript for a book filled with "all the words God had given her." When she attended her first writers' conference, a kind editor took the time to assure her that she had, "A lot of little gems in that book." While the manuscript remains in a bottom drawer, she has pulled the gems from it to use for other writing opportunities.

Her writers' conference experience inspired her to help organize several different conferences. "It was more about helping other writers than getting published at that point," she says of her experiences. During that time, she got involved with the "Write To Publish" conference, serving as the assistant director for six years. Her job allowed her to meet and get to know many editors and other contacts in the publishing business, which she found highly beneficial.

Carla's writing experience grew out of diverse opportunities. She did a lot of work-for-hire assignments, including writing *The Children's Discovery Bible Devotions* for Cook Communications and several puzzle books filled with hands-on activities for children. She also wrote numerous articles for magazines. "These experiences," she says, "gave me lots of bylines and presented me with new challenges."

In the midst of her writing jobs and involvement with conferences, Carla also lived a busy life ministering with her husband and raising their children. "For four years, I was the marching band 'mom' in charge of 150 uniforms," she remembers fondly. "Now that was a big job!" Carla also found herself increasingly volunteering in her children's schools. Blending her passion for writing with her desire to remain active in their schools, she taught writing on a volunteer basis. This expanded to a paid position, teaching writing workshops in ten schools. She received a grant and developed a program to instruct teachers how to teach children to write. "I wanted to blend the rules of writing, which they needed for state testing, with the fun of writing," she says.

Throughout all of this, Carla continued to develop and re-write a book on parenting that she carried in her heart for ten years. Just as her family geared up for a major move to another state, the book, *As You Walk Along the Way,* was accepted for publication. Simultaneously another book proposal, *My Bible Dress Up Book,* was also accepted. "There was a time," she remembers with a laugh, "if you came to my house you either helped with packing or sewed Bible costumes!"

Just as her dream of being published was realized, Carla found that helping her family adjust to the move and supporting her husband in starting a new ministry inhibited her from developing as strong a platform as she would have hoped. The issue of developing a platform is one that all writers must deal with at some point. Carla found herself, like many writers, in a Catch-22. "Publishers want you to have a large platform when you come to them, yet it is difficult to build a platform without a book. To build a platform, you almost have to have a book or resource of some type in your hand. I found it much easier to land speaking engagements once I had a book."

The publisher allowed *As You Walk Along the Way* to go out of print, but Carla wisely bought all the remainders from them. WinePress Publishing (located in the town she had moved to and her husband's publisher) provided her a new ISBN and warehousing for the remainders. "I knew I could sell the book at my book table when I speak," she explains.

In addition to publishing eleven books in the traditional market, Carla has helped her husband Tim self-publish twelve books and numerous tracts. Her relationship with WinePress has grown into the position of Editorial Director for the company. "I helped set up guidelines for the editing part of the process," she says. "I constantly look for editors who can keep our editorial standards high." Too often, self-publishing has been linked with poor editing, and Carla strives to change that. "Most people come to self-publishing new to the market and in need of good editing. They may have a book on their hearts, but lack the skills required to put out a quality product." In addition to her position with WinePress,

Carla also serves as the president of the Northwest Christian Writers Association and directs the Alaskan Christian Writers Cruise.

Over the years, Carla has found that writing articles can provide great experience. She remembers a time early in her writing career when she took a book proposal to CBA. "An editor told me to prove I had a market for a book I had proposed on teaching spiritual disciplines to children. I knew I could market the idea through my speaking, but additionally I decided to write an article based on the book. I sold it to *Christian Parenting Today* and when they surveyed their readers on the topic, many wrote in saying they would like more information on this subject. Well, that proved I had a market for the book!"

Carla also reflects on a more recent time when she was planning a double wedding for her sons. "It was a very stressful period," she recalls. "I couldn't really take on too much writing at that point. For eighteen months, God provided an opportunity for me to write 350-word monthly assignments for *Focus on the Family's* parenting inserts. It was a great experience pulling out old ideas and trying new ones and perfecting my writing skills. I wrote on teaching kids prayer, worship, hospitality and things like that. I was grateful for the experience at a time when I could not have done much else."

Carla's heartbeat has always been to teach children to love God with all their hearts. When she and her husband married, they decided not to establish priorities in their marriage. There would only be one: fulfilling the greatest commandment to love God with all their heart, soul, mind, and strength. "If we did that, we knew all the other priorities would fall in line. I have learned that it's not about getting published, but about obeying God in everything, especially teaching children to love God and fulfilling His purpose for me by doing so."

In the last five years, Carla has concentrated more on speaking than personal writing. As she looks to the future, she sees herself venturing back into the traditional publishing market along with continuing to self-publish. "I'm ready for a new challenge," she says. She maintains two web sites: thewritessence.com and newdayministry.org. Her whole family—including her two married sons—minister together and she enjoys this new phase of her life.

"When I started in the ministry with my husband, I was only 24 years old," she recalls. "Although expected to have all the answers, I didn't have a clue. Now I gladly share the mistakes I made along the way. I have earned my gray hair," she jokes. "I love being an older woman and sharing what God has taught me. I still have more to learn about writing and more to write about, but the key is obedience to His call."

Carla Williams, author, speaker, and workshop leader, has writing credits in curriculum, devotions, short stories, activities, games, and numerous articles in many publications. She has authored or coauthored over twenty-three books, including *As You Walk Along the Way: How to Lead Your Child Down the Path of Spiritual Discipline, My Bible Dress-Up Book,* and *Ears to Hear.* At the printing of this book, she is serving her fourth year as president of Northwest Christian Writers Association. *www.newdayministry.org*

Never Too Young, Or Too Old

Read I Timothy 4:12, Jeremiah I:6-8, Job 12:12, Job 32:6-9

For many years, I used the excuse that I couldn't write or speak because I was too young. I felt that people wouldn't take me seriously and I still had some livin' to do before they would! Then one day I stumbled across 1 Timothy 4:12 and realized a simple but truly life-changing Truth. God uses people of all ages to reach others. He doesn't look at age. God does not qualify us based on the number of years we have lived, but on our level of commitment.

Perhaps you are reading this thinking, "I only wish I was too young! I'm too old for God to use me." Job 12:12 assures us that nothing could be further from the truth. We would all do well to be like Caleb, who at age eighty-five was ready to go out and fight for the Lord. Joshua 14:10b-11 tells us, "So here I am today, eighty-five years old. I am still as strong today as the day Moses sent me out; I'm just as vigorous to go out to battle now as I was then."

Truly, God calls all ages, from all different walks of life to do His work. We can not offer the excuse of being too young or too old, as He has proven in His word that He will use whom He pleases, when He pleases. All we really need is a heart that is sold out for Him.

Ask God today to help you have a heart that is fully committed to Him, no matter what your age or limitations may be. Thank God that He does not discriminate according to age!

Discovering My Gifts Within

By: Micca Campbell

English was my worst subject in school. I hated it. Who cares what a participle is anyway? That was my attitude, and it showed in my grades until a new semester changed our lessons from grammar to writing. Suddenly, my disappointing "D" soared to an awesome "A." Being a drama queen meant that storytelling came easy to me. I still didn't know how to label my sentences correctly, but as one teacher remarked, "I could express them in a way that you could smell, touch, taste, and feel."

I never thought much about my writing. To me, the skill only helped balance my most challenging subject so that I made a better grade. Otherwise, I stuffed my gift deep within.

When I turned eighteen, people suddenly expected me to use my talents to change the world! There was only one problem. I didn't have a clue what my talents were or how to use them.

I knew I wasn't the sporty type. I had tried that. My last name carried a lot of weight being the younger sister of an all-star athlete like my brother. When I signed up for softball at the community center, the coaches actually fought over me until they learned I couldn't play. Then, they traded me to another team. It was clear. Sports were not my gift.

I had also tried following in my sister's steps by taking piano lessons. That didn't go well either. The teacher told my mother that I was the only child she had ever encountered who came to class knowing less than the week before. That's because I despised playing the piano. I would sit on the bench in our living room and dream about safari hunts in the back yard or bobby-pinning a yellow bath towel to my head, transforming myself into a princess with long blond hair. I could concentrate on many things, but not little black notes. They would trickle right out of my head.

That was then. Now was my time to make a contribution in life. "What could it be?" I often asked myself. Maybe I had missed my giftedness in music. I did enjoy singing even though most of my songbooks seemed to be defective and written off key. Perhaps now that I'm older, I have magically developed athletic skills. I am a good dancer even though I am Baptist. Frustrated about the subject, I decided to discuss it with my mother.

"Mom, do you think I have any talents?" I questioned sadly.

"Of course you have talents," she replied with confidence.

"Do you think my gift was playing the piano and I missed it?" I asked.

"I recall you begging to quit. You told me it was ruining your life. Anyone who knows that at the age of eight doesn't have a love for music," said mother.

"Then what am I good at?"

With wisdom, my mother confirmed, "Your gift is within. You just haven't found a way to express it yet, but you will."

I married, experienced tragedy, married again, and birthed three children before God pulled from the depths of my soul a gift that He would use to affect others and bring me great joy and satisfaction.

It's a day I'll never forget. For fifteen years I had been a student of God's Word. Like any other day, I retreated to my bedroom chair to meet with Him. This day was to be different. In our regular meeting place, the Lord called me to surrender my life to full-time service. I don't claim to have heard the audible voice of God, but it was the loudest thought I ever had. At the time, I didn't know what it all meant, but I responded wholeheartedly to God's plan for my life.

Part of the Lord's plan was to place me with Proverbs 31 Ministries. While God was opening doors for me as a speaker, I never dreamed I would become a writer as well.

It began one day when Mary Southerland asked me to join her in writing a weekly devotion for the Proverbs 31 Speaker Team. In the position of Director, Mary felt it was important to encourage the team both personally and spiritually. To Mary, it was no big deal. Her plan was for us to alternate weeks, and I was to go first! I felt many emotions with this unexpected invitation. I was honored, of course, but mostly I was afraid until my fear eventually turned to panic!

"I can't write! I can't even spell!" I shouted to my husband.

"Who signed you up to write devotions?" he inquired.

"Mary did. Apparently, she thinks I can write," I explained with fear and trembling.

I knew this was going to take a lot of discussion that could throw my willing, but not "created to talk about it for hours" husband into overload. Once again, I called my mother.

"HELP! I have to write a devotional," I urgently explained.

"That's wonderful," mother replied with joy.

Confused by her remark, I wondered if mom had heard me correctly or not. She had.

"Micca", she said. I knew when she began her sentence with my name that mom was about to say something important. "You are focusing on what you can't do instead of what you can do," she said in such a way that I recognized the tone and could see her expression in my mind's eye. "Time after time, you have been commended by your school teachers, collage teachers, and even your seminary professor on your writing style, not your grammar. This is the way you are to express your gift. It's what you've been waiting for. It's time to write," mom said proudly.

God uses mothers in so many ways . . . to comfort us, teach us, encourage us, and to discipline us. That day, God used my mother to open a world of dreams I never thought possible.

Are you like me, seeking the confidence and reassurance to let go of your fears and step out in faith? Then allow me to share some nuggets of truth that I hope will become stepping-stones into your future of writing.

First, you don't need to be good at grammar to be a good writer. Sure, there are those that love the art of dotting every "I" and crossing every "T", but we don't all share that passion. Besides, if we were all good at grammar we wouldn't need editors. People need people. God created us that way. He will place in your life a person with strengths where you are weak to balance your gift. Ask God to provide you with such a person. Someone is longing to come alongside of you and use his or her gift as well.

Second, don't try to copy the technique of anyone. You are uniquely designed. God didn't create you to fit in, but to stand out through your own style. You have a specific way of communication through writing. Find your voice by simply writing letters to your family and friends. The way you express yourself in common everyday experiences is your individual voice that reflects your own method. There are many writers, but your style is one of a kind.

Third, the key to writing is . . . revise, revise, and revise again. Don't ever expect your first draft to be your final copy. Striving for perfection the first time around will cause you to struggle for words. Begin by writing whatever comes to your mind. Then, go back and revise. Shorten your sentences, add some adjectives, and write in your transition sentences. For words that are repeated often, use your thesaurus to find a different word with the same meaning. It will make your writing more interesting.

Writing is like any other gift in that it has to be practiced. If God is not opening doors right now for your talent, don't let it become dormant. Keep writing, so that when the time is right, you are ready to step through that open door into a world of expression where words are countless, dreams are real, and possibilities are endless.

> "Not that we are adequate in ourselves to consider anything as coming from ourselves, but our adequacy is from God."
>
> —2 Corinthians 3:5

Micca Campbell is an author and speaker with Proverbs 31 Ministries. Her passion is to know God and be one with Him while leading others into that same kind of relationship until all become complete in Christ.

Using Your Gifts

Read Jeremiah 1:5, Galatians 1:15-16, 1 Peter 4:10-11

C ould God have called me to write and to speak for Him?" I wrote this question across the top of a page in my journal several years ago when I first felt these stirrings in my heart. As God sent confirmation through His word and His people, I recorded these events and scriptures in my journal. Before I knew it, I had filled up several pages and discovered an unavoidable answer to my question.

As I look back over my life, I realize that God certainly did have a purpose in every trial and at every turn. What I saw as random and unrelated was God's amazing tapestry being woven together in my life. He truly did set me apart, blessing me with specific gifts and challenging me with certain weaknesses. He did all of this to prepare me to serve Him by doing my part within the Body. He put His words in me so that they could pour forth from my pen and from my lips.

God has set you apart, too. Notice that the verse in I Peter says, "Each one." We have all been given a gift to use for God's glory. Are you letting your gift shine for all to see—or are you hiding it under a bushel? Don't make the mistake of burying your talents in the name of modesty, fear or self-doubt. Confidently step out in service to the Lord, according to your unique gifts, and trust Him to show up in a mighty way. He is there, believing in you, cheering you on, willing you to have the courage to pursue your calling.

Think back over your life. Record specific events that you long to share. Now record specific talents or gifts that God has given to you. They are there, waiting to be unearthed and put to use. Pray over this list, thanking God for your experiences and your gifts!

The WinePress Story

An Interview with Athena Dean

I n the late 1980's, Athena Dean worked with a ministry that decided to publish a book. The Executive Director had written the book to use as a resource all over the country but could not find an interested publisher. Someone stepped forward and agreed to walk them through the complicated process of self-publishing. They printed 10,000 copies of their 150-page book for $1 per book and sold all 10,000 copies over a two-year period. Shortly after that, Multnomah picked up the rights and, over the next eight years, sold 40,000 copies. Because of their publishing success, other people began soliciting their help with self-publishing and WinePress Publishing was born.

As WinePress has grown with the Christian publishing industry, Athena has observed many trends and fluctuations in the market. She stresses the importance of understanding the market. "Some of what goes on can depress you," she says. "But knowing this keeps you from thinking there's something wrong with you!" Athena points out seven major trends currently playing out in the Christian publishing industry:

1. Publishers want celebrities or recognizable names that generate guaranteed sales. Authors with an established track record of bestsellers drive the book market.
2. The numbers simply do not favor an unpublished author. Most publishers receive 500 to 5000 unsolicited manuscripts per month, yet only publish 10-120 books per year. Thomas Nelson, for example, cut its list by half and other publishers are producing 10 to 20% less titles a year. The percentage of writers taken out of the slush pile, or unsolicited stack, remains very low.

3. Books only make up 25% of sales in a typical Christian bookstore. Therefore, two-thirds of the shelf space goes to music, cards, and gift items, which leaves very little room for non-bestselling authors.

4. Publishers have found that it takes just as much work to sell 200,000 copies as it does to sell 10 to 20,000. For that reason, they have little interest in selling a mere 10,000 copies when they can sign someone that will sell 200,000. They would rather produce fewer titles with higher sales than many titles with decent sales.

5. Secular companies own many of the larger Christian publishers and therefore look at the financial bottom line. They have shareholders to answer to who want to see a profit. In such cases, unfortunately, ministry has been exchanged for money.

6. The Christian market follows the trends of the secular market. Athena says, "If something is hot in the secular market, more than likely six months later you will find it in the Christian market with the name of Jesus tacked on. It's sad, but that's the trend."

7. You can still find some good Christian publishers and other viable alternatives for getting into print. Self-publishing has grown in reaction to the shrinking of publishers' front lists.

Athena states, "Our goal at WinePress is to assist you in getting the message God has given you into a printed form that readers can get their hands on." The self-publishing process falls into one of four categories:

1. Self-publishing on your own where you do all the legwork and assume all of the responsibility.

2. Self-publishing with a professional custom publisher like WinePress.

3. Print on demand (POD) on your own—like at Kinko's®.

4. Print on demand with a professional publisher. WinePress' POD division is called Pleasant Word.

No matter which avenue of self-publishing you choose, this route provides the following advantages:

1. You are guaranteed publication. Your book will be in print if you self-publish.

2. While profit should not be your focus in ministry, you will make more profits from self-publishing. Athena gives the example of the book the ministry she worked for did. They sold 10,000 copies over two years and made $40,000. When Multnomah

bought the book and sold 40,000 copies, the ministry made about $20,000 in royalties.

3. You can establish a track record for your book by first self-publishing and testing the market. Some authors do this as a stepping stone before going with a traditional publisher. In fact, quite a few authors have utilized WinePress to prove their market and have subsequently been picked up by traditional publishers.

4. You retain the fun and creativity of the hands-on production of your book. "Once you sell your book to a publisher, it's no longer yours," Athena says. "In self-publishing, you have input on every aspect of the book—from cover design to content."

5. You have editorial control of the book's content. Athena tells of one author who went to self-publishing after a major publisher removed his main strong points because they could have caused waves.

6. Self-publishing offers a much faster turnaround time. Traditional publishers usually take about 18 to 24 months (one year in rare exceptions) to place a book on the market, while self-publishing takes about 3 to 6 months. Many authors have found this aspect invaluable when preparing for a major PR event or speaking engagement or when capitalizing on the timeliness of a current event, like 9/11 for example.

7. Self-publishing teaches you to think like a publisher. You gain a new appreciation for the publishing process by going through all the steps. You know firsthand what it takes to get a book into print.

Athena is a stickler for a good, quality book. She advises authors to choose their cover carefully and says, "People *do* judge a book by its cover—whether it's professional looking. The packaging needs to really grab the reader if you want people to take you seriously." She adds that the book shouldn't *look* self-published and cites examples she has seen of ugly covers, words crammed on a page to lower the page count, even one book that was written in all capital letters. She goes on to point out additional pitfalls one should avoid when self-publishing:

- Poorly written back cover copy and author bio
- Unprofessional author picture
- Poor editing and proofreading
- Books that are unavailable to traditional and online bookstores
- Publishers without a presence in the Christian market (some of the bigger secular print-on-demand publishers offer decent services but have no presence in the Christian market making your book unavailable to Christian bookstores).

Athena clearly loves what she does and has a passion for helping other people spread their messages. "Did you know that self-publishing is actually in the Bible?" she asks excitedly. She flips open her Bible and reads, "Publish His glorious deeds among the nations. Tell everyone about the amazing things He does," (Psalm 96:3, NLT). WinePress Publishing provides Athena a way to help authors do exactly what that verse says, and do it with excellence.

Athena Dean has been helping Christian authors become published for over fourteen years. She has built WinePress Publishing from a small home-based business into the leading Christian custom publishing company with over 1,000 authors in print. She currently serves as treasurer for Northwest Christian Writers Association and is the author of *You Can Do It, A Guide to Christian Self-Publishing; Consumed by Success;* and *All That Glitters is Not God.* She is also the author of a free monthly e-zine entitled You Can Do It! Market & Promote Your Book. *www.winepresspub.com athena@winepresspub.com.*

Being Willing To Go

Read Matthew 4:18-20, I Kings 19:19-20

Once you know that God has called you to write and/or to speak, what is your next move? I tried the "sit and wait" approach for awhile, thinking that if God had called me into ministry, He would also send opportunities my way without me having to do anything. As I read God's word, however, I saw the opposite view being presented. Time and again, God's people responded to His call by being willing to GO—to take immediate action as a response to their encounter with Him.

Jesus did not run His ministry by sitting inside His house waiting for people to find Him. He was active, moving from place to place, inviting them to take part in His Father's business. Jesus became my model for how to approach ministry. I stopped sitting in seclusion, waiting for ministry to begin and went out in search of the hurting people who need to hear words of encouragement and hope.

Where are you right now? Are you waiting or taking action? One thing I noticed about both of the Bible passages for today is that none of the people involved seemed to hesitate or count the cost of leaving behind what was familiar. They felt God tugging at their hearts, dropped what they were doing, and went off to fulfill whatever He had planned. They were ready to GO. Are you?

Elisha dropped his plow. Peter and Andrew dropped their nets. What do you need to leave behind so that you can GO out and fulfill God's call on your life? Write down anything God brings to mind. Pray and ask God to show you three action steps you can take this week to begin to further your ministry and fulfill your calling. Write these down and commit to take these steps as soon as you can.

Use Me Lord

By: Terri Clark

Sitting in my hotel room looking out the window, I can't help but be in wonder at God's hand in my life. I have walked through doors surely meant for women more deserving than myself, speaking to women around the country, traveling to places most people only read about in National Geographic, and actually writing and publishing a book! I'm sitting here wondering if God somehow got me mixed up with someone else. How did all this happen?

I think it all started back when I was in one of those special, quiet times of one on one communion with God. I whispered three little words, "Use me Lord." I had no idea what kind of door I was opening. I'm not sure how it all happened, but since those words fell from my lips, my life has changed dramatically. God took me seriously!

I wanted to be used by God and fulfill His call on my life, but I wasn't even sure what that call was. I am, after all, just an ordinary woman—an Arkansas homemaker, mother of six kids in a blended family. But, one willing step in faith at a time, God began to unfold his plan for me.

There I was, a Christian women's speaker and teacher struggling to apply God's principles to my own Brady Bunch, frustrated with the hard emotional issues of blending a family. As God gave me direction and answers from His word in my home, I felt compelled to write about it. Who knows, maybe the things God was teaching me would help other families one day. The idea of putting all those years of journaling and learning into a book was born.

Forcing me to step outside my comfort zone into the twilight zone, those three words, "Use me Lord," kept me at my computer for days on end writing and re-writing until I felt certain the words on the page were exactly right, and then changing them one more time. I wasn't even sure what I would do with the pages I was writing, would anyone even be interested?

"Use me Lord." Those three little words drove me to talk to editors—even after I heard they ate authors for lunch. What if they found out I've never written anything before? Would they spit me out and send me back to Arkansas?

After taking that initial, knee-knocking step into the world of acquisition editors and publishing houses, I made a remarkable discovery—they were human just like me! I presented my idea to an editor for Broadman & Holman Publishing and he liked it. With an open door in front of me and an invitation to walk through it, my book, "Tying the Family Knot," was on its way to becoming a reality.

Since then, Terri Clark Ministries, Inc., a non-profit corporation has been formed, "Tying the Family Knot" seminars and workshops, based on my book are encouraging those in blended families in America, and my speaking ministry to women has grown internationally to include annual mission trips to Africa.

So I sit here in my hotel room, overlooking an African city, in awe of God's hand in my life. When I ask Him, who am I Lord, that you would use me? I hear Him whisper in a still, small voice, "Just an earthen vessel containing the treasures of heaven willing to be poured out for My glory" (2 Corinthians 4:7). God is using me, not because I am unique or different from any other woman, but because I asked Him to.

> . . . let us run with endurance the race that is set before us, fixing our eyes on Jesus, the author and perfecter of faith . . .
>
> —Hebrews 12:1-2

Author and popular speaker, **Terri Clark** inspires women in retreats and conferences across America and abroad. Her book, *Tying the Family Knot* encourages those struggling with step-family issues. Additionally, Terri's ministry tangibly shares God's love by building a medical clinic and educating children in Uganda, East Africa. For more information on Terri Clark and her ministry, visit her web site at *www.terriclarkministries.org*.

Here I Am, Lord

Read Genesis 22:1-2, Genesis 31:11, Exodus 3:4, Isaiah 6:8-9, I Samuel 3:4

When God whispers your name, beckoning to you, how should you respond? As we read these accounts of Old Testament heroes being called by God, we find one commonality. Though they were all called to different actions, they all responded with the same reply: "Here I am." Seeing how God used these servants has inspired me to answer the same way—with these three simple words packed with transforming power. When we stand before God and boldly proclaim "Here I am, Lord, your willing servant. Use me for your glory," we should be prepared to be amazed.

I will never forget standing at a Mercy Me concert as they sang very similar words. The Holy Spirit was evident in that place. Lifting my arms toward Heaven, I sang along with all my heart, "Here am I, send me." I wanted to go to the ends of the earth for Jesus, and I left the concert with a renewed passion for proclaiming His light in a dark world (1 Peter 2:9). I still can not hear that song without feeling that sense of renewal in my commitment to Christ.

God does not call all of us to go to the ends of the earth. For some of us, our ministry will be found in our own backyard—reaching the lost in our community, our neighborhood, even just in our own family. It is one thing to share Christ with a total stranger you may never see again. It is another thing entirely to witness to those who know you best. And yet, that may be exactly what God is requiring of you. So the next time you hear God whispering your name, answer Him and say, as Samuel did, "Speak Lord, for your servant is listening" (1 Samuel 3:10). Listen to what He tells you; then determine to obey it, no matter what.

Do you have a song that inspires you in your walk? It could be an old hymn, a praise and worship chorus, or a popular contemporary Christian song. Write down the title, and then listen to that song throughout the coming week. If you are ready, tell the Lord, "Here I am." Write in your journal about this time between you and the Lord.

The Muse Does Not Exist

By: Sandra P. Aldrich

Recently, I told my aunt about my latest book. She chuckled, then said, "Honey, I wish I could just sit down and write!"

I wish I could, too! Even after 17 books, writing is still hard work for me. So, if it's hard, what keeps me at my desk? Well, I am compelled to write. I can't NOT write.

Oh, I wish I were one of those ethereal types who can stare at a cloud then write a best-seller. But my style is more about REwriting than writing. I seldom get it right the first—or the third—time. But along the way, I've learned this calling demands perseverance as well as talent. After all, I think of the times I've read something and thought, *I could have written that*.

What's the difference? That author wrote. I thought about it.

My son, Jay, graduated from college with a friend who planned to write the Great American Novel. But several months later, the friend took an entry-level job. When Jay asked about the book, his friend shrugged.

"I'm waiting for the Muse."

Jay looked at him for a long moment. "Come over to my mom's house some night when she's on deadline and she's typing with tears running down her cheeks because she's so tired. Then I'll show you the Muse."

When Jay reported the scene to me, I hugged him. He understood: only real effort produces real results.

Oh, I have days when I wish I *could* beckon a muse. Instead, I'm forced to keep hitting the computer keys until something readable appears. Apparently, I occasionally get it right because I've won several writing awards and serve as a writing mentor for thirty- four apprentices for the Jerry Jenkins Christian Writers Guild.

Here are some of the ideas with which I try to encourage those beginning writers:

Since God has called us, He already has equipped us. First Corinthians 1:7 says, "Therefore, you do not lack any spiritual gift as you eagerly wait for our Lord Jesus Christ to be revealed." The Message puts it this way: "Just think—you don't need a thing, you've got it all! All God's gifts are right in front of you as you wait expectantly for our Master Jesus to arrive on the scene for the Finale."

With that encouragement, we don't dare think we can't answer our calling. Think of it this way: Every time we beat ourselves up and say we can't possibly accomplish what we want—and need—to do, we're helping the Enemy. He loves it when we give up. After all, if we tell ourselves we can't write, we won't get the Good News out to a hurting world desperately looking for hope.

Invite God into your work. Yes, He has equipped us, but He still wants to be part of the process. Starting each project—and even each page—with a simple prayer not only opens wells of creativity but reminds us that He alone is our Source. And remember the most profound prayer is just one word: "Help!"

Don't get it right—get it written. We can always tweak the phrases after we get those first few words on paper—or the screen. Worrying about the project wastes energy. The worse part of any job is dreading it. So jump in.

For those times when the first sentence refuses to come, I start a pretend letter: "Dear Mother, today I'm trying to write an article about the effects of..." and before I know it, I have my lead.

Yes, grammar counts. Beginning writers often think editors are just sitting at their desks, sipping lattes and longing to rewrite tomes filled with bad grammar. But from my years in the editor's chair I know the countless articles rejected because of grammar problems getting in the way of the message. Why should an editor choose a sloppy manuscript when she/he has a stack of professional ones from which to choose?

One new writer, not wanting to take the effort to learn basic grammar rules, argued such action wasn't fair.

"Wouldn't the editor be concerned with the details?" she asked.

"Yes. Concerned enough to choose another article" was my realistic reply.

Don't be afraid to start small. My first magazine article was a 500-word filler purchased for $30. And even though relatives dismissed the importance of that little article, I knew my publishing journey had begun.

Life gets in the way sometimes. Children get sick, relatives decide to visit. But if we wait for the perfect time, we'll find it's like the nonexistent muse—it doesn't show up. I finished my first book back in 1982 when my young husband was dying of brain cancer. I gladly would have forsaken the project, but he said he wanted to see the manuscript completed before he died. When I met that goal, he sent me flowers and thanked me for not waiting.

Use your past in your writing. In what way have your experiences shaped you? I was born in Harlan County, Kentucky and have often wondered what route my life would have taken if I had grown up surrounded by folks who loved me. But that wasn't to be since my family became part of what the sociology books call The Great Migration into the northern states. Michigan did not want the influx of southerners, but we had no other place to go. So, we dug our heels in, worked hard—and reached our goals.

No one's journey is easy. In fact, some days the only thing that keeps me going is my personal faith in the Lord and my own innate stubbornness as to the calling on my life. How about you?

How badly do you want to write? What is keeping you from the fulfillment of your dreams? Tough circumstances? Other people? If you are compelled to write, you can't listen to those voices. I'm evidence dreams do come true. And if my dream of writing books and reaching thousands of people each year came true for me, so can yours! But it starts with the determination not to give in to the discouraging predictions, but to follow the set-jawed voice within that says, "I *will* win!"

So here I am—saying, "Don't you dare quit!" Keep writing, keep moving toward your dream, and one of these days it will come true. And you will be able to credit God and your hard work rather than some nonexistent muse.

Sandra P. Aldrich, president and CEO of Bold Words, Inc. of Colorado Springs, Colorado, is a popular speaker who presents life's serious issues with insight and humor. She can be reached at *BoldWords@aol.com*

Stopping Satan

Read Mark 4:13-20, I Thessalonians 5:19

You have heard God's voice, recognized your calling, identified your unique gifts and talents and said yes to God. You are ready and raring to go. You are filled with joy, with peace, with unrestrained passion. You have discovered your true purpose and your life is finally perfect. Right?

Wrong.

Often, by the time you reach this point, you are exhausted, overwhelmed and battling defeat. You spend your days waffling between being sold out for God and being terrified. The further you get out of your comfort zone, the more you find yourself longingly looking backward at your old life. You know Satan is prowling around your door, asking to sift you like wheat (Luke 22:34), and you do not want to give him any victories. You know that his desire is to snatch the word away from you and to steal your joy.

Satan desires to quench the Holy Spirit within you by stifling your ministry any way he can. One very real, unavoidable result of saying, "Here I am," to God is that Satan hates to hear those words, and will go after anyone who utters them. His chief goal is to stop us from serving God so that others can not come to know His saving power. To say, "Here I am," is to enlist in a battle. I'll never forget being at a conference when the speaker arrived. As he approached us, he got a big smile on his face and said, "Has Satan been on the attack today?"

Grimacing and groaning, we confirmed that he had indeed been working overtime. "Good!" he said. "That means God is going to do something big here this weekend! That is just what I wanted to hear!" Through airport delays, book shipment problems, and low turnout, this man did not allow Satan to put out the Spirit's fire. May we all be prepared to do the same in our own ministry!

Where is Satan attacking you specifically? List these areas and pray over them. Ask God to bind Satan and to prepare you to stand in the battle. When you are able to overcome Satan, give God the glory!

Called to "Bee" a Writer

An Interview with Thelma Wells

Thelma Wells' first book wasn't on the Bible or women's interests. Far from what you might expect, Thelma Wells wrote her first book on banking. A banker by profession, she partnered with an attorney to write a procedure manual on the rules for new accounts in the state of Texas. "Though I don't really consider that to be my first book," Thelma says, "Writing it did give me encouragement that I was capable of writing things people could understand."

Thelma left banking to develop her speaking career in 1984. Shortly after this change, she was sitting in her office at home one day when she began to draw a rainbow on yellow paper. "Now, you must understand," she says, "I don't draw. I can't draw a straight line with a ruler. But for some reason, I began to draw this rainbow. I felt God telling me at that time that I was going to write a book. I came out of my office and told my husband, 'I'm going to write a book.' And he said, 'Okay baby, you can do that.' I still didn't know how or when it was going to happen at that point. I just knew I had heard from God."

Several years after this, the National Speakers Association scheduled Thelma as the keynote speaker for their national convention in Dallas, Texas in 1993. She says, "When they called my office and asked that my books be at the speaking location within the next six weeks, I was shocked and wanted to know if having a book was a requirement for a keynote speaker? My daughter, Vikki, who was working with me, took the telephone, got the details for the book to be delivered, told them it would be there on time, hung up the telephone and informed me, in no uncertain terms, that I would have a book ready! My question to her was, 'What book?' She informed me that I had been procrastinating for too long. I could write the book on what I was talking about at NSA. My instructions from her were to write the book on planes, in hotel rooms, and wherever I could. Then I was to fax the manuscript to her and leave the rest up to her. Little did I know that meanwhile she was researching the proper size, spine design, illustrations and finding a book printing company. She succeeded in getting 1800 copies of *Capture Your Audience Through Storytelling* completed and at the venue on the desired date. I call it 'My 30-day Book.' We sold nearly all 1800 copies that weekend. And I had written my first book!"

After that first book, Thelma met Dr. William Spence, who owned a publishing company in Waco, Texas. Dr. Spence asked her about writing a second book. "I already wrote a book," she told him. "I don't have anything else to say." Dr. Spence pressed further, insisting that anyone who had lived at least fifty years had something else to say. "I considered myself very ordinary," she remembers. "I wondered who would want to hear from me." Thelma met a writer who could help her write the second book and they met weekly for 18 months as they explored stories from Thelma's past. "We dove deeply into the past and many things—some painful—surfaced." Thelma still considers the book that came from that time, *Bumblebees Fly Anyway,* to be her signature book.

The title for the book came from an experience Thelma had one Sunday morning. "I was going into church and I had on this bumblebee brooch. It didn't mean anything to me, I just thought it was pretty," she explains. "A lady at my church commented on my brooch and said, 'Thelma Wells, just remember every time you wear that pin, you can bee the best of what you want to bee.' " Her friend's comment really stuck with her so Thelma went home and began studying about bumblebees. She learned that, aerodynamically, bumblebees aren't supposed to be able to fly. Their bodies are too heavy and their wingspan is too shallow. And yet, the bumblebee does what God intended for it to do.

Thelma got excited as she noted the spiritual lesson the bumblebee provides. She remembered something someone had said to her many years before: *If you don't know where you're going, you won't know when you get there.* "He inspired me to move from mediocrity to excellence and that is what I wanted to do for my readers. The bumblebee was a great example of that. We can overcome disillusionment and disappointments in our lives. God has given us everything we need to knock down barriers and overcome obstacles, just like the bumblebee. That theme has transcended all my books and all my speaking."

After the release of her second book, Thelma continued to ponder the obstacles she had overcome. She realized that she had personally witnessed countless small miracles in her life. "People call them 'situations' or 'circumstances' or 'coincidences,' " she says. "But I don't believe that. I believe we have divine appointments every day." She began writing down those everyday miracles, along with scriptures and affirmations to back them up. "I had learned the power in speaking positive affirmations to myself in the first person, present tense. These aren't 'I will' or 'I did' statements. These are 'I am' statements." Thelma gives examples like:

I am well and healthy.
I can do all things through Christ who strengthens me.
I have all the money I need to do everything I need to do.

As she began pulling this together, her daughter ("That same bullheaded one.") encouraged her to write another book. She showed what she had to an agent, who confirmed that she had the makings of another book. The agent was able to land her a three-book contract with Thomas Nelson.

While Thelma was thrilled with her contract, she was also nervous about being able to write three more books when she really only had enough material for one book. One day she was driving to the airport with her agent when she saw two rainbows up in the sky. Though at the time she did not remember drawing that rainbow in her office, she was moved to tears at the sight of those rainbows. Her agent asked her why she was crying. "I don't know why," she choked out, "But there is something significant about those rainbows." Out of that experience came the title for the first book for Thomas Nelson, *God Will Make A Way.* "My sainted grandmother raised me and brought me to Christ at four years old," she says. "And she always used to say to me, 'Honey, God will make a way.' "

Thomas Nelson split that first book based on everyday miracles into two books. The second book was titled, *What's Going On, Lord?* and left her with only one book needed to fulfill her contract. But the third book did not come quite so easily. She had been taking notes and keeping lists of the hurts and issues women had been approaching her with when she spoke. "These women are dealing with grief, divorce, health issues, job concerns, time management, abortion, alcoholism, you name it. I came up with a list I called 'The 43 Woes of Hurting Women.' I wanted to write something based on the Bible to help these women deal with their struggles."

After months of wrestling with this book, Thelma was ready to throw in the towel. The book was not coming together and in frustration, Thelma called her agent. "I'm not going to be able to do this," she told her. "You'll just have to work something out with Thomas Nelson." Her agent spent time praying with her and challenging her to persevere. "I started praying: Look God, if You want this book written, You better write it Yourself. I told Him I was giving it one more month and I was through. I was tired." She laughs at the memory. "Oh, I'm glad He doesn't fall off His throne when we act crazy."

One morning at 5:13 am, God woke Thelma up. "The Spirit of God in me said, 'Write it like you talk.' I realized that I had been trying to write like an authority. I was trying to write in somebody else's voice and it wasn't working. I got up right then and went to my computer. In two weeks, I had that book finished." Using letters she had received from women, Thelma was able to write the book as though she was answering letters. The book, *Girl, Have I Got Good News For You,* fulfilled her three book contract with Thomas Nelson.

Thelma's biggest role right now is speaking with the Women of Faith conferences. She began with them in 1996 after she got a call from a woman who wanted to meet with her about speaking for an unnamed woman's organization. At the time, Thelma was already speaking 300 times a year and did not need to take on another commitment. "Besides," she told the woman, "I don't like women. They're petty and jealous. I've resigned from every woman's organization I've ever been a part of." The woman asked her just to come to three events to see if she would like it.

She remembers walking into the green room and meeting Barbara Johnson, Marilyn Meberg and Patsy Clairmont for the first time. "I remember thinking, these ladies are crazy. They're not like regular Christians—they're not stuffy and churchy. There was an immediate bonding." Thelma was still not convinced that she should become a part of Women of Faith. "So, I told the woman I would look at my calendar for the coming year and if even one of their dates wasn't available, I wasn't going to do it. Do you know, out of twenty-seven dates, not one was a conflict? God had cleared my calendar! I told Him, 'OK God, I will bloom where you plant me.' "

Since that time, Thelma has only missed two Women of Faith events. "I don't want to miss a single time," she says. "I'd miss the laughter. We have so much fun. I never get tired of hearing the messages because I hear something different every weekend. Those ladies have become my family. We're even all living in Dallas now. I thought I didn't need Women of Faith, but I did. This experience has expanded my faith outside of my little world. Through my contact with the other speakers and the attendees I meet, my faith has grown."

Thelma just released a new book, *The Buzz: Seven Power-Packed Scriptures To Energize Your Life*. Another book, co-written with Carol Kent, *Kisses of Sunshine For Women,* is forthcoming. To date, Thelma has written, co-authored, endorsed or written the forward for over 300 books. She also runs a leadership training program called Daughters of Zion, teaches for the Master's Divinity school and leads a Bible study once a month for twenty people. "I look at everything I have going on and I say to myself, 'Girl, you've been busy!' " Thelma is also married, the mother of three daughters, grandmother of nine, and great-grandmother of one. "The best part about my life is that in the middle of all I have going on, I still have time to write. Every morning I ask God to give me inspiration. I ask God not to let me waste time. And I ask God to order my day, and He does. Life is wonderful."

With upbeat, joyous enthusiasm, popular author, speaker and businesswoman Thelma Wells offers affirmations of God's watch-care over us, and assurances of His personal intervention and direction in our lives in her books *Bumblebees Fly Anyway, God Will Make A Way, What's Going On Lord?, Girl, Have I Got News for you!*, and *The Buzz-7 Power Packed Scriptures to Energize Your Life.* From angels protecting her on a busy freeway in Texas, to suffering abuse and neglect in a dark closet as a child, Thelma has learned that in the lean times, the mean times, the blessed times and the stressed times, God is faithful. Thelma is a speaker for the Women of Faith conferences. Learn more about Thelma from her web site, *www.thelmawells.com*.

Nothing To Hide

Read I Timothy 1:5

After my marriage fell apart, it was a long time before I could talk about it with anyone. When I did try to share my story, I would begin to physically shake all over. I was not ready to share something so hurtful, even though a happy ending was part of the story. I needed time to heal, and God graciously gave me that time. Slowly, I noticed that I was able to talk about it more easily—at least my teeth did not chatter anymore! I knew that God wanted my husband and I to be willing to share our story with other hurting couples. I knew we could offer hope and understanding.

Too many of us fear being real and sharing the ugly parts of our lives. We think that our story is too personal to share with others—and it is personal. Just don't make it private. The world is looking for people who are authentic, transparent, and, well, messy. They survey the wreck of their own lives and compare themselves to what they mistakenly believe is perfection in others' lives. They don't seek perfection, though. They seek sincerity, according to 1 Timothy 1:5—a real, transparent faith that is without hypocrisy.

What story are you hiding that you have prayed you would never have to share? We all have one or two. We fear revealing who we really are, and Satan holds that fear out before us—paralyzing us with it, and preventing us from reaching the lost and hungry people who need to hear the very story we would like to hide.

What is the one thing you don't want to share? You can write it down, or not. Pray and ask God to ease your pain, to equip you to share it if He asks, and to set you free from your fear and Satan's snares.

Successfully Living for God

An Interview with Kendra Smiley

It could be said that Kendra Smiley's entire writing career grew out of her desire to avoid dusting. A teacher with a master's degree in education, she was earning more than half of the family's income when she quit teaching in 1978 to stay home with her firstborn, Matthew. "Of course, to all my highly educated friends, I was throwing away my education just to be a mom. That was something you just didn't do back then. But for my husband and I, there was never a question."

As Kendra settled into her life as a stay at home mom, she made a startling discovery: stay at home moms are expected to dust. "Between school and a career I had pretty successfully avoided that up til then, so this was a new pressure in my life," she remembers. As an effort to avoid dusting and to provide some adult interaction in her life, Kendra started a home-based business with a direct marketing company called Successful Living (no longer in business) which sold Christian books through home parties. "I really didn't make much money at it," she remembers. "But I made enough to take the kids to McDonald's every once in awhile and to support both my husband's and my serious book habit and provide books for the kids."

Looking back at that time, she can see God's hand was already at work. Through the company's national convention, Kendra was able to meet Christian authors like Kevin Leman and James Dobson. As her boys grew and started school, Kendra expanded her business by taking the books into Christian schools and selling them in the classrooms. "I really felt like it was a ministry," she explains, "To bring life-changing books to people and introduce them to these wonderful authors."

As Kendra presented her book programs in the community, she had people begin to ask her to come back and speak on other topics. After speaking to different groups for awhile, she had a lady ask her a question that revolutionized her speaking: How much do you charge? She was amazed that someone would actually pay her to speak. One opportunity led to the next as her speaking ministry grew.

Meanwhile, Cook Communications purchased Successful Living and hired her as a consultant to help organize their next national convention. Unable to come up with an appropriate title for her position, they let her choose one. So she called herself "the fun chairman." "How great is that?" she asks excitedly. "Now that was a job I was born for!" As part of this job, she was asked to find and hire speakers from the Christian publishing industry to speak at the convention. Her challenge was to find speakers that not only had a great message, but could articulate it as well.

One of those authors was a lady named Gwen Ellis. The two connected through several phone conversations. During one particular conversation, Gwen asked Kendra about her position and it came out that Kendra was also a speaker. Interested, Gwen asked Kendra to send her tapes of her messages. After listening to Kendra's tapes, Gwen asked Kendra another question that would change her life: Have you ever considered writing a book? As Kendra pondered that question, she realized she had always had a desire to write but lacked the confidence. "Even back then—and it's worse now—publishers really didn't take unsolicited manuscripts," she says. She expressed her concerns to her new friend. Gwen assured her that the publishing side was already under control. To Kendra's surprise, Gwen revealed that she was the senior acquisitions editor for Servant Publications and she believed they could make something happen.

Gwen became Kendra's editor for the project and walked her through the entire process. "She was such an encourager. When I wanted to give up, she would tell me I could do this. She was my cheerleader, really. It was truly a gift from God for that to be my first experience with publishing." The book, *Empowered By Choice,* was released in April and by CBA in July, it had sold 13,000 copies. By August, Kendra had signed a contract to write two additional books for Servant: *Give Your Heart A Good Spring Cleaning* and *Happy Kids Make Good Choices*. In the meantime, Cook Communications contracted with her to do a gift book for Mother's Day. In a very short amount of time, Kendra had gone from merely considering writing, to becoming the author of four books.

As her speaking and writing exploded, she started a one-minute radio program to be broadcast across her home state of Illinois. As she began to expand the program into other markets, she sent a demo packet to Moody Broadcasting in Chicago. When she did not hear anything back, she made a follow-up phone call, only to discover that the man who had received her packet had left and her demo was missing. She called an acquaintance at Moody, who assured her that she would personally get a new demo to the right people.

Though her demo did not result in her getting on Moody's network, it did result in a phone call from Moody Publishing. The demo had made it to their department and they had liked what they heard. They wanted to know if she had a book on her heart that she wanted to write. She told them about a book idea based on her experience as a stay at home mom running a home-based business. Moody contracted her to write the book, *High Wire Mom*. They also re-released her first book under a new title, *Empowering Choices*. Her most recent book for them, *Aaron's Way*, was released in April 04.

During this time, she was also contracted by Cook Communications to write a book called *One Rehearsal Christmas Plays*, a book that came out of her years of experience at putting together simple Christmas plays for her small country church. "These plays aren't stressful to put on," she explains. "You can glorify God and still be smiling when the production is over."

In seven years, Kendra has now written seven books, something she wouldn't have attempted when her boys were smaller. Her sons are all grown now, and she looks back on her time at home with them as a treasured time. She recalls hearing one of her sons on the phone as he was telling a friend about something he had done with her. "As I eavesdropped on that conversation," she says, "I was struck by how much my role has changed. 'Mom' used to be my job description, now it's a term of endearment."

Kendra challenges mothers to make sure their children know they are important—more important than any job or commitment. "If you are in the stage of raising a family, then now is the time to invest in them," she says. "I think it is a trick of the Enemy to convince us we are trapped in the season of life we are in and we'll never get out of it, so we better do what we want now. Had I forfeited the energy I poured into my sons, I doubt they would have turned out the way they have."

Many times when Kendra speaks, a woman will approach her and say, "I want to do what you do." Kendra realizes that her life as a speaker and a writer looks fun and intriguing, especially to a young woman in need of an outlet and some adult interaction as Kendra herself once was. She always hesitates to advise anyone who asks her how she got her start because, as she says, "My story is not reproducible. What do I say? Oh, get hired as a consultant and make friends with an acquisitions editor you don't know is an acquisitions editor and then let her convince you to write a book?" she laughs. "What is reproducible about my story is to give your heart and life to the Lord—strive to do that with all that you are—and try to understand exactly where He wants you to be every step of the way."

Kendra admits that people have other misconceptions about "doing what she does." "They tell me, 'Well I just wish I had control over my schedule like you do,' " she says. "In reality, the only thing I have control over is my ability to say no. I have learned to keep family first and not let a really good speaking engagement take priority. It's about making smart decisions. I used to worry that they wouldn't like me if I turned them down, but then I realized that the people booking me are not the people who will be visiting me in the nursing home, so I shouldn't worry so much what they think."

One of the ways that Kendra has learned to make smart decisions is by having key people in place to help her make those decisions. One of those people is her husband of thirty-two years, John. When describing him, she says, "He is just one of the most incredible human beings I have ever met. He inspires me to be a better person just by observing how he lives. I often say that he is the brain and I am the voice. He really deserves his name on every book I've ever written."

The other key person in her life is her manager. "Can you believe I have a manager?" she laughs. "I mean, I'm a mom!" Her decision to hire a manager came out of her need to have someone manage her career. "After my youngest son left for college, the phone started ringing off the hook and my schedule was really filling up," she says. "I wanted to make smart choices as to how to best fill my schedule from the opportunities I had in front of me." Though she interviewed several agents, none of them offered what she was looking for. "They wanted to offer more contracts and bigger contracts, but that's not what I was wanting to hear from them. I needed career guidance. My manager has been able to give me that by opening doors I didn't even know were there. I write his check every month and say, he deserves every cent."

Kendra speaks internationally for both Christian and secular groups. When speaking to a secular group, her philosophy is, "not to scare them with scripture but to tantalize them with the truth—Jesus Christ. God has shown me favor and it works because people are looking for Truth. I tell my audiences that all of my books are inspirational, so if you do not want to be inspired, then don't buy them. I used to have on my cds: 'Great Physician's Warning: This product contains scripture. It may change your life'."

Kendra tells of a letter she received from a lady who had been in one of her secular audiences and bought one of her books. The woman boarded the plane to head home and opened her new book to read during the flight. When she saw that it was a Christian book, she almost closed it. She reasoned that Kendra had been funny and engaging and she would go ahead and give the book a try. The letter ended in saying that, as a result of that book, she had been saved, her husband had been saved, and they were both being baptized that weekend. "I mean, that's why we do what we do, right?" Kendra says excitedly. "That's what it's all about." Another life changed by the willing heart of one of God's servants, who is still managing to get out of dusting.

Kendra Smiley is an author, speaker, and radio host. A former Illinois Mother of the Year, she makes her home on the family farm in Central Illinois. Her most recent book is *Aaron's Way: The Journey of a Strong Willed Child*. A sought-after speaker, Kendra helps people make the next right choice. For more information, check out her web site, *www.KendraSmiley.com*

Sharing Our Scars

Read John 20:24-28, Isaiah 61:1, John 8:32

When Jesus appeared after the resurrection, He appeared bearing the scars from His crucifixion. Let's think about this: He is God. Therefore, He could have re-appeared in any form He chose. He could have stood before His disciples in total perfection, not a blemish on His body. "He could have come back ten years younger," quips Kendra Smiley. But He chose to come bearing the scars left from the suffering He had endured. As writers, and as Christians, how is this an example to us?

We should be unashamed of the scars we bear from our suffering. Perhaps our scars aren't visible to the eye. Perhaps our scars are the more painful kind we keep hidden in our hearts. These scars are not the scars we want anyone to ever see. They are the marks of shame and rejection, secrets and fear. Jesus also suffered agony, humiliation and rejection, but He did not hide what had happened to Him.

What scars can you show through your writing and your interactions with others? What truths—however painful—can you share with those who need to make a decision for Christ? When Thomas saw Jesus' scars, it made all the difference. What kind of difference will it make to those you encounter?

Is God calling you to tell the truth and to share your scars? Do not be afraid to follow His leading so that more and more people can find freedom in Christ.

Pray Isaiah 61:1, committing your message and your ministry before the Lord. Define your purposes according to the truths in this verse. Record any revelations God gives you during this time of prayer. Consider posting this verse somewhere so that you can meditate on it throughout your day.

* Special thanks to Kendra Smiley, whose words to me inspired this devotional.

Do It Yourself!
A Self-Publishing
Success Story

• •

By: Rebecca Ingram Powell

It began as an ordinary Sunday school class, but within a few minutes of hearing Sondra's prayer request, God handed me a writing assignment.

"I want y'all to pray for my brother," she drawled, as only Southerners can do when sharing a concern. "He started boot camp and it's terrible! He only gets around five hours of sleep each night, and he has to wolf down every meal. He doesn't have time for anything, and his drill sergeant is always yelling about something!"

To me, her brother's ordeal sounded eerily like new motherhood—no time to sleep, no time to eat, someone always screaming—and Sondra, who had just announced her first pregnancy, would be facing similar circumstances in less than eight months. Would she be prepared for the boot camp of motherhood? I remembered my first days as a mom. I wondered if the experience might have gone more smoothly if I'd had someone around to cheer me on. A desire was planted in my heart as I realized I'd love to be there for Sondra, every day of the first six weeks, if I could. That very afternoon I began writing what would be my first published book, *Baby Boot Camp,* a collection of devotionals designed to encourage and support new moms through the challenging first six weeks of motherhood.

Actually, writing books was not new to me. Publishing, however, seemed to be an unattainable dream. I began working on my first novel, a book for pre-teen girls, right after college. I sent it out to several publishing houses and waited months at a time for each rejection to finally arrive, bringing closure and the permission to start again. When my babies came along, I gave up chasing publishers and willingly surrendered my dream, counting motherhood my greatest ministry and my home my most fertile mission field. When my husband and I made the decision to homeschool, writing seemed like something I would only be able to do once my children were grown.

But incredibly, when I began writing *Baby Boot Camp,* God provided a couple of quiet hours every afternoon. The baby napped, my older children played together, and within six months I had a manuscript ready to pitch. My sister read it and immediately sent it to a friend of hers who worked for a large Christian publisher. Unbelievably, without a formal proposal, it began going through the channels.

Several months later, the book went to the final decision-making meeting. There, the sales force determined that *Baby Boot Camp* wouldn't sell. They felt that new mothers wanted "warm and fuzzy." They didn't think a book about "surviving" the first six weeks of motherhood would be appealing to most women. Besides that, I was an unknown author with no platform and no guarantee that I could sell my book. So they passed on *Baby Boot Camp,* and a gracious editor called me to gently break the news. It hurt.

I had a message of hope for young moms, and I wanted to get it to them. My husband and I began exploring the options available through self-publishing. I learned that self-publishing is a wonderful alternative for new authors. I contacted WinePress Publishing and within a couple of days I received a call from the publisher, Athena Dean. She loved my book and believed other people would, too. The only problem now was the money. That's the one drawback to self-publishing. You have to put up the money on the front end. Once your book starts selling, however, you keep the profits!

I needed $15,000 to publish 5,000 copies of *Baby Boot Camp.* One night, as my husband lay in bed praying about this project, he told the Lord, "We don't have the money." He heard the Lord's still, small voice reply, "I don't need your money." So, believing that God would provide, we actually signed the contract with WinePress and began the procedure having no idea where the money would come from. But the Lord knew.

Two weeks before the first payment was due, a couple in our church came to us with a check for $5,000. God had spoken to the husband and the wife separately. They came together realizing what they were to do. They hadn't even read the manuscript! But they believed in being obedient to God. When another payment was due, God handed us the money again. The book was published, and as it began selling, the people who invested in this dream were repaid. They didn't expect or even want their money back. But I wanted to be obedient, too.

How did I sell that self-published book? Even my mother had mentioned that self-published authors often wind up with garages full of books they never sell. (Publishing houses do, too.) Here are some tips to get you started selling and promoting your book.

Establish a web presence. Yesterday's business card is today's personal web site. A web site serves as your storefront, publicity desk, and mailroom. You'll be directing people here to learn about you and purchase your book, so be sure to have a site that looks professional. Research author sites online. Obtain a domain name in your own name or the name of your book. Secure the talents of a techie friend or a qualified webmaster and get started!

Online reviews. Some self-publishing companies can get your book listed on sites such as amazon.com. When your book is up (and what a thrill that is!), immediately send an e-mail to your friends and family asking them to write a quick review.

Freelance writing. Freelancing is the most effective way that I found to promote my book. Many publications offer the decided benefit of a short bio with your byline where you can list the name of your book and your web site. Is your book about parenting? Begin investigating parenting magazines. Start by offering an excerpt from your book as an article.

Develop your message into a speaking topic. I know, I know—perhaps you don't want to speak. How passionate are you about your message? If you really believe in it and you want people to read your book, you need to develop a speaking ministry. Sell your books from a resource table everywhere you go to speak.

Once I had sold over half the books, I began to approach traditional publishing houses. Clearly, the book was marketable. I now had a platform, having acquired a monthly column in *ParentLife* magazine and by making myself available as a speaker. *Baby Boot Camp* soon found a home with New Hope Publishers and was re-released in January 2004. Today, the book continues to be a favorite shower gift as well as an outreach tool for churches eager to reach young families. God continues to open new doors of ministry for *Baby Boot Camp,* now also being used by military chaplains as they strive to minister to thousands of new moms whose husbands are deployed in the Middle East.

Would I self-publish again? You bet! In fact, my latest project, *Wise Up! Experience the Power of Proverbs,* a Bible study for girls becoming women, has just been released through Pleasant Word, a division of WinePress. Benefits such as creative and editorial control, as well as a faster turnaround time and a higher profit margin, drew me back. No matter what you decide to do, self-publishing or traditional, one thing that does not change is that you still have to promote your book. You must be willing to aggressively market your book, believing in what you have to say and knowing other people can gain from it. No one will be as passionate about your message as you.

Rebecca Ingram Powell is a wife and homeschooling mother of three, a monthly columnist for *ParentLife* magazine, and the author of *Baby Boot Camp* and *Wise Up! Experience the Power of Proverbs*. She speaks on a variety of topics including self-publishing, writing for magazines, and Christian parenting. Contact her at *www.rebeccapowell.com*.

Wait Loss

Read 2 Peter 3:8-9, Isaiah 30:18

There are times in our lives when we must wait on God. The problem with waiting is that none of us *like* to wait. We discuss the quality of a doctor's care based on whether we have to spend too much time in the waiting room. We compare notes on how to avoid standing in line at the Department of Motor Vehicles. We try to patronize restaurants that offer "call ahead" seating. In our society, we do not see waiting as a beneficial experience.

So how can we learn to trust God's sovereignty and His timing? As we wait on Him to move in our lives, we must actively practice laying down our wants, our demands and our timetables at the foot of His throne. We must exchange our agenda for His, and truly seek to learn whatever lesson He is trying to teach us through this time of waiting.

I have heard it said before that God is rarely early, but never late. As He shows up in what we might think is an eleventh-hour rescue, He shows us He had it all under control—and His resolution is oh, so much better than we could have ever orchestrated ourselves. Are you waiting on God right now? Perhaps you are waiting for financial or physical healing. Perhaps you are waiting for healing in a relationship. Perhaps you are waiting for God to reveal His plans for you and give you some direction. Or maybe you are waiting for God to open doors for your writing.

The scriptures today reassure us that God's timeline is perfect, but His timetable will probably not match ours. He has a purpose in His timing. It helps me to remember that He always works things out so that others will come to know Him. And that is worth waiting for!

What are you waiting for? Write it down. As God allows this time of waiting on Him, how can you take advantage of this opportunity to grow in your understanding of Him? To become more Christ-like? To help others come to know Him through this experience?

An Agent's Perspective

An Interview with
Janet Kobobel Grant

Janet Kobobel Grant has been in publishing all of her professional life. She started out as Director of Publications for Campus Crusade, then moved to Cook Communications as an editor. From Cook, she moved to Zondervan as an imprint editor, then landed at Focus on the Family as Managing Editor of Books. When Focus moved from California to Colorado, Janet made the decision not to go with them. Instead, she assessed what she most enjoyed about her job and concluded that was helping authors to become successful. As a result, she decided to develop a literary agency to manage the careers of authors. So, in 1997, the Books & Such Literary Agency was born.

The agency turned out to be the perfect niche for Janet. She enjoys being in the background, shining the light of success on the authors she represents and helping them spread their message to as broad an audience as possible. In her prior publishing experience, she had already developed a strong network of contacts and had experience with negotiating contracts. God used all these factors to add up to an equation that she could never have envisioned working out so beautifully.

Currently, Janet has about fifty clients that she represents. Her client list reflects a careful balance of both established and new authors. She has found that an agent who can strike that balance is seen as more valuable to publishing houses. Publishers often turn to agents, Janet notes, to help them work through the slush piles on their desks. When they are looking for a new voice that is exciting and fresh, they go to the agents for help. Therefore, Janet does find it beneficial to represent new authors, while her established clients help maintain her reputation in the industry.

Janet has a series of questions she asks herself when she is considering a new client. After she has reviewed a sample of his or her work and read through a proposal, she asks:

- Has this person been published before?
- Does this person have a lot of good ideas or just one? Since Janet is primarily interested in helping writers develop careers, she is more likely to be interested in someone who has many ideas that can be developed over time.
- Is this idea marketable? Janet looks at the kind of sales potential the idea has before taking it on.
- Does the idea have broad appeal? Books that cater to a very specific market typically do not appeal to publishers, which Janet must consider. She gives the example of a book on a specific childhood illness, which would only appeal to parents of children with this illness. However, a book on parenting children with a variety of challenges, whether they are chronic illnesses, mental handicaps, or difficulties in developing social skills, would appeal to a broader range of people. In this way, the same basic idea has now been expanded to broaden its focus.
- How many publishers are likely to be interested? A good agent knows what publishers are looking for, and what directions the publishers are headed in.
- Can I enthusiastically sell this person as well as this project? Janet's favorite authors to represent are those she can tell a publisher, "Not only do I have a great project for you, but I have a great author for you."
- Do I feel genuine excitement about this proposal? Janet stresses that agents are basically salespeople. The focus of their work is always, "Can I sell this to a publisher?" Selling is all about enthusiasm. If she lacks enthusiasm for a project, it will affect her ability to sell it.
- Finally, Janet asks, is this person a fantastic writer? One thing Janet has learned is that if you are a fantastic writer, you will get published. Period. "There comes a time when it is not about manipulating the system just to get published," she says. "The best way to get published is still to simply write a really good manuscript."

As an agent, Janet serves as an advocate for the writers she represents. "An agent," she says, "is the center point in an ever-changing universe of the publishing world." Publishing houses get bought out, editors leave, but your agent stays with you throughout your career regardless of what house you're with, what genre you're in, etc. The agent helps you make transitions, offers career advice and gives direction as to where to send your work. An agent sees you through the entire life of your book and helps it go out of print gracefully when the time comes. Generally, writers are not thinking about these elements when they sign a contract, but an agent can help think through the many contingencies found in contracts that a writer may not be aware of.

Of course, contract negotiation is a large part of an agent's job. Agents know what houses can be difficult to work with, which houses are slowest to pay, which ones are the least financially stable, and who can pay the most money. The agent can also help an author determine what he or she is worth. Janet says, "Authors are typically unsure as to how much they are worth, and are so thrilled to get a contract that they accept anything. They feel unworthy to ask for more." A good agent will not only help you determine your worth, but will also tell you what that publisher can afford to pay. An agent will also make sure that the publisher lives up to the obligations it agreed to. Indeed, the business side of writing can be complicated for writers. Janet notes that when she opened her agency in 1997, a contract averaged about four pages long. Currently, the average contract is about fifteen to twenty pages long.

A relationship between an agent and a writer is like a marriage. Consequently, finding just the right agent is crucial. Janet advises that writers ask lots of questions before they sign with an agent. She points out that there are *bad* agents out there, and a bad agent can do you "more harm than good." An ineffective agent, for example, will send proposals to publishers that are not a good fit for the project, negotiate contracts haphazardly, and leave your work to languish on their desk for months, wasting your precious time. Therefore, Janet recommends asking a potential agent the following questions:

- Why did you become an agent? The answer will tell a lot about an agent's motivation.
- Have you successfully placed projects like mine? Ask for specific examples.
- What kind of working relationship do you prefer to have with your clients? Some agents want to deal strictly with the business side of publishing while some enjoy being involved in the creative process.
- Do you prefer going after the biggest houses and the most money, or do you also build relationships with smaller publishers?
- What are your expectations from your clients?

Janet also recommends asking for references from the agent's clients. She cites again that agents are sales people and will have no problem selling him or herself to an inquiring writer. Clients are more likely to tell you about both an agent's strengths and weaknesses. Later, it will be up to you to decide if you can live with what you have heard.

Finally, Janet recommends that all writers who are just getting started should stay busy while attempting to find an agent and a publisher. "Above all," she says, "Writers should constantly hone their craft." She recommends taking classes at a local community college or joining a writing critique group. She also advises using the time to develop a speaking ministry. She suggests writing magazine articles as a way to gain both writing experience and credentials. It surprises her when someone who has little to no experience with writing decides to write a book. "To me," she says, "that's like deciding to climb a mountain before you have ever climbed a hill!"

In her years in publishing, Janet has seen God at work in both her career and the lives of the many authors she has worked with. She has watched Him close some doors and miraculously open others. She feels blessed to be a part of His plan for these writers and to help them spread their message to others for His glory.

Literary agent **Janet Kobobel Grant** represents several best-selling authors and winners of the Gold Medallion, Christy Award, and RITA. She has been an agent since 1997 and before that was an imprint editor at Zondervan and managing book editor at Focus on the Family. Also a writer, she has collaborated on 17 books and written two books of her own. A recent collaboration was *Every Child Needs a Praying Mom* with Fern Nichols, which was a Gold Medallion Finalist in 2004. Janet knows the publishing world from the perspective of a writer, an editor, and an agent. She has written a booklet available on the web at *www. kickstartcart.com/app/aftrack.asp?AFID=139516*, which tells in much more detail about the world of agents and how to find one. Her web site is *www.janetgrant.com*.

Trusted Counsel

Read Proverbs 2:6, 13:10, 15:22, 20:18

Part of deciding to pursue Christian publishing is to realize that, while you are embarking on a great ministry opportunity, you are also going into a business endeavor. Part of that business will involve making wise decisions—financial, career and otherwise. It is evident in the scripture for today that anytime you face these types of decisions, it is always best to seek God's face first and then to also have people in place that can serve as wise and godly counsel.

These people may include a mentor, a family member, an agent or a friend. Make certain that you identify these people before it comes time to make big decisions. Never try to "figure it out for yourself" or carry the burden alone. That is not what God intended. If you do not have anyone in your life to provide wise advice, first of all, pray. Ask God to send that person to you. Also, consider hiring an agent to serve as a trusted source of counsel. Of course, God will certainly act as your agent first and foremost by opening doors and giving you supernatural guidance. But sometimes you may really need a person to bounce ideas off or provide career direction. It is okay to need that. It is actually Biblical. Learn to ask for advice—and learn to take it, for this is part of gaining wisdom.

The book of Proverbs is full of verses on the pursuit of wisdom. Using your Bible concordance, jot down some more verses on wisdom that speak to you.

Speaking and Writing According to God's Purpose

An Interview with Naomi Duncan

As coordinator of women's events for the Ambassador Speakers Bureau, Naomi Duncan deals with the connection between writing and speaking every day. She coordinates events for approximately 100 speakers, most of whom are also published authors. She has found that the main connection between writing and speaking is the credibility that a book gives to a person. The book helps them build a platform to then speak from. Books give exposure and help authors become more widely known. "I can think of several gifted communicators who have definitely been limited in their speaking by not having a book," she says.

Naomi explains that some speakers are simply not as gifted in the area of writing. "Usually people are stronger in one area and have to work at the other," she says. "Though there are definitely exceptions who excel at both. Frank Peretti, for example, is just a gifted storyteller—whether speaking or writing." Naomi points out that being good at storytelling is the one element that helps bridge the gap between being an effective writer and speaker. Kevin Leman is another storyteller who does a great job with both writing and speaking. He knows how to be entertaining and engaging using humor and stories.

An obvious advantage of speaking is that it enables the author to promote their books. Naomi has noticed a cycle: "The more you travel and speak, the more you can promote the book. The more the book gets promoted, the more demand there is to travel and speak." She cites several examples from Ambassador's roster of popular speakers:

- Andy Andrews is a motivational speaker and entertainer. His book, *The Traveler's Gift,* was turned down over thirty-one times by publishers. However, when it did get published, it became a New York Times bestseller. Why? For him, it was a matter of God's timing. Because it was published right after 9/11, the country was eager for the book's message.

- Lisa Harper was on staff with Focus on the Family. Her position there led to speaking, which ultimately led to publishing. She first published two books with a smaller publisher, then signed with a larger publisher. She now has a four-book deal with them. For her, the key was being willing to take baby steps to get her to where she is.

- Shaunti Feldhahn got her start when she published a book on Y2K. She felt that God had told her to spread this particular message. Of course, it was very time-specific and faded away quickly. After that book, she published two novels. Through these experiences, God ordained several connections that led to the publication of her book, *For Women Only*. This book's impact and interest has grown rapidly and has led to many speaking requests.

Naomi says that most of Ambassador's speakers come from referrals from other speakers or from event coordinators they work with. "These people give us the best recommendations because they know us and they understand who fits with our way of thinking and what we do. It is not very often that we seek someone out." Naomi adds that every agency has their own way of doing things, which means that not every speaker is going to be a good fit for every agency.

Because she deals with primarily women's events, Naomi has a good feel for what coordinators are looking for. "More and more, I find that they want real, authentic people who bring a concrete message. They don't want fluff. They aren't looking for just a testimony and some entertainment. Bible teachers—people like Beth Moore—are in demand."

The speakers at Ambassador are typically not beginners who are just starting out. They are the people who have been speaking for awhile and have built up to a certain level. Some of them may only do one event every other month and some of them are out three to five times per month. "That just varies between each speaker," Naomi says. "Some of them have another full time job or family demands that keep them home more. But for some of them, this is their full time job and they want to be out as much as possible."

Speakers' fees are another area that varies greatly. Ambassador's speakers are generally at the level of at least $1000 per event, but most earn between $2500 to $4000 per event. Naomi notes that figuring out what to charge is difficult for most every speaker. "One of our speaker's friends had such a good perspective on that, though," she says. "People aren't just paying for that one hour you speak. They are paying for the hours and years you have spent studying, learning and preparing to speak. They are paying for your expertise and your background. We don't hesitate to pay a doctor's fees because we know part of what we are paying for is their years of schooling to become an expert. I think it is the same with speakers."

In addition to preparation and expertise, another element to a speaker is their passion for what they speak about. Naomi stresses that being passionate helps people to understand you and to connect with you. She recommends that any writer or speaker should take time to analyze what they are passionate about—not just the topic, but the intention behind it. Ask yourself, *Why do I want to write this book? What does God want to do with this book?* You may think you know where God wants to take you, but sometimes He has a bigger purpose and plan than we can imagine. "Don't presume to know God's purpose," Naomi says. "From what I've seen, the things He blesses more are the things that have His glory and purpose behind them. Rest in His bigger picture and always do what will glorify Him the most."

Naomi Duncan is coordinator of women's events for the Ambassador Speakers Bureau in Nashville, TN. She is married and the mother of one little girl.

The Writing/Speaking Connection

Read Psalm 45:1, 2 John 12, 1 Timothy 4:13, 2 Corinthians 11:6

I love to write. It feels very natural to me to express myself on paper. I realize that this is not true of all people. Some people are better speakers. I struggle with speaking and find getting in front of a crowd to be downright unnerving. There are probably two types of people reading this book—writers who become speakers and speakers who become writers. (I do realize that there are those rare exceptions that enjoy and excel at both!) The fact is, in the Christian marketplace, both are necessary for spreading the word to potential readers. Publishers are very likely to ask a writer, "Do you have a speaking ministry?" And speakers are very likely to hear, "I loved your message, do you have a book I can read?"

In our verses for today, we read that God is well aware of the speaking/writing connection. Jesus traveled all over, speaking to people. He was the greatest communicator that ever lived. But when He left us to join His Father in Heaven, He left us His Word—preserved for all to experience in His absence. Both elements were necessary for the spread of Christianity. The Apostle Paul met with people in person, preaching and teaching the gospel message. When He could not be with his beloved people, however, he wrote letters—letters that still offer encouragement and instruction to us today. In Matthew 24:35, Jesus said, "Heaven and earth will all pass away, but my words will never pass away." There are two ways to spread His precious word—speaking and writing. Let's not neglect either as we seek to further God's Kingdom.

Read Psalm 96:3. There are two ways to declare His glory and tell of His marvelous deeds. Which feels more natural to you? Ask God to grow you in whatever area you feel weakest by providing you with opportunities. Remember your prayer as He brings opportunities your way. Write down what happens and be sure to thank Him for this chance to grow!

Speaking and Writing with Confidence

An Interview with Carol Kent

There are writers who speak and speakers who write. I would definitely consider myself a speaker who occasionally writes," says Carol Kent. "Of course, I've written a lot of books, so I guess that sounds funny for me to say."

By profession, Carol Kent was a teacher who specialized in alternative education programs for pregnant teens. Because she came to know the Lord at age five and grew up as a Christian, Carol says it was natural for her to bring all she knew about the Lord into the classroom. Because of her unique experience with pregnant teens, she was given her first opportunities to speak.

When her son was born, Carol began a small Bible study with a few neighbors who met in her home. Then she and her husband moved to Fort Wayne, Indiana. She was invited to become the Director of Women's Ministries at Dr. David Jeremiah's church, and on the first day of Bible study, 225 attended the class that was held at the church. All too soon, her husband got a job transfer and the family moved to Port Huron, MI. "A place I was convinced was the back side of the spiritual desert of the world!" Carol remembers. Not long after she moved, a neighbor called to ask her if she would consider leading a Bible study for the women in her neighborhood. The woman told her that they had about 30 women who had been praying for a Bible study teacher before she moved there. Before long, Carol and her friend, Sherrie, launched a Bible Study Fellowship class that soon had over 350 registered participants.

Through that Bible study, Carol noticed that there were several women with wonderful testimonies who lacked the confidence and the skills to share their stories publicly. Taking what she knew about public speaking from teaching school and her own public speaking experience, she developed a three day seminar for those women called, "Speak Up With Confidence." "About fifteen women came to that first seminar," she remembers. "Now I do about eight to twelve seminars all over the United States each year and have even traveled internationally to present this training."

Since Carol's main focus was on speaking, writing was not even on her radar screen when a woman approached her after one of her Speak Up seminars. The woman explained that she had a good friend in publishing and was going to tell him about the seminar. This woman believed that the seminar material Carol was teaching had book potential. A few days later, she got a call from the woman's friend—Michael Hyatt, then Vice President of Thomas Nelson. He told her to send him a proposal for the book. She hesitantly admitted that she had no idea what a proposal consisted of!

With his help, she was able to put together a proposal and, within a few short weeks, she had her first book contract. "That was a divine appointment only God could have orchestrated," says Carol. "My story makes it sound easy, and I don't want to make it sound that way. I was a rare case in that, while I had taught English and knew about writing, I had never even written an article for a periodical before I got my first book contract!" That book, *Speak Up With Confidence,* is now in its tenth printing and has been used as a speech text in Christian schools and universities. "Though it certainly wasn't designed to be a textbook," she says, "I love how God is using the book."

After that book, Carol began brainstorming with her editor to do a book on helping women to overcome deep disappointments and unfulfilled expectations. "We called that book, *Secret Passions of The Christian Woman,* and it was printed in hardcover under that title. The title with the word 'passion' in it made the publisher nervous, though. Of course, the world hadn't met Mel Gibson and discovered the power of that word yet!" she laughs. The book was eventually reprinted in trade paper under the title, *Secret Longings of The Heart.* One of her recorded messages on the content of this book was featured on Dr. James Dobson's Focus on the Family radio show. This particular show has been re-broadcast numerous times, and served as a springboard for future ministry. "That show really opened doors for my public speaking," she says.

Through Carol's extensive writing and speaking experience, she has gained a lot of godly wisdom to share with those who come behind her:

1. She asks herself, what one new thing this year do I want to become an expert on? Sometimes these are subjects she already knows about. Sometimes they are subjects that require a lot of research. This yearly challenge keeps her broadening her mind and sometimes leads to new subject matter for writing and speaking.

2. Writing is hard work. People want it to be easier, but it requires hard work, discipline, and sacrifice. She says, "There are people who are depending on you to fulfill that contract, so you can't just say, 'I got too busy.'"

3. You need to speak or write according to your passion in life—not just to get in print.

4. When Carol's son was young, a woman approached her after a speaking engagement and asked accusingly, "So, who watches your son when you speak?" "That question burned a hole in me," she remembers. That day, Carol realized she had many years to pursue her dream, but only a short amount of time to be with her son. She now challenges mothers to really evaluate what season of life they are in, and act accordingly.

5. Start where you are with what you have. "If you are a stay-at-home mom right now," Carol says, "Start by leading a home Bible study. I am so glad that God let me start with that. He didn't open doors right away for a national ministry, and I wasn't ready for it."

6. If you want to minister to women, you must first ask yourself: Do I love these women? Love is an essential ingredient for ministry to be effective and transformation to take place.

7. When speaking or writing, be very intentional about your desired outcome. You should be working towards a desired change in attitude or behavior that is measurable. If not, then your aim is still too vague. "Many people aim for mere inspiration or motivation," Carol says. "But we should aim for transformation."

8. "Prayer must permeate the process," she stresses. "I am in a pray-without-ceasing mode in my life right now. I pray with my eyes wide open because I am praying all the time."

9. People will always ask you to do more than God asks. She quotes Alan Redpath, who said, "Say yes to the burden that God puts on your heart and say no to everything else." A whole lot of things can wait for a different season in your life or even for just a different time of year.

10. In times of stress, Carol lists the five most energy and time-consuming things in her life and prays over them. She then asks the Lord to show her what of these things could be delegated to someone else in her life. Many times, God shows her someone already in her life that is glad to take on that task or responsibility.

Carol stumbled into publishing through God's divine opening. "God did it in a most amazing way," she remembers. Because of her Speak Up seminars, she comes in contact with many women who would like to write or speak. "They want to know how you break into publishing, how you find the right agent, how you create promotional materials," she says. "But really, you should be focusing on your relationship with the Lord and on His agenda. He'll do the rest."

Carol Kent is a popular international public speaker best known for being dynamic, humorous, encouraging, and biblical. She authored the bestselling books, *When I Lay My Isaac Down* and *Becoming a Woman of Influence* (NavPress). Her messages have aired on Focus on the Family and she is a featured speaker at many Women of Faith arena events. Carol is the president of Speak Up Speaker Services, a Christian speakers' bureau, and the founder and director of Speak Up With Confidence seminars, a ministry committed to helping Christians develop their communication skills. For information, call 888.870.7719 or go to *www.SpeakUpSpeakerServices.com*.

Keeping Our Word

Read Joshua 9, Numbers 30:2, Matthew 5:33,37

In Joshua, we read the story of Israel and the Gibeonites. When Israel began defeating all the kingdoms in the Promised Land, the Gibeonites got scared and tricked them into signing a peace treaty. This treaty ensured their safety and protection from Israel, even though it was drawn up under false pretenses. In the end, the Gibeonites' clever ruse became a snare to them as they were forced into a life of servitude to the Israelites. When Joshua learned of their deception, he allowed them to live because he had given them an oath before the Lord. This passage is important because it illustrates how seriously we should take the oaths we make before God.

In Joshua 9:14, Israel's biggest mistake is made clear. The men of Israel sampled the Gibeonite's provisions, "but did not inquire of the Lord," it says. A lot of confusion could have been avoided had Israel taken the time to seek God's direction before they signed any treaty or made any oath. This illustration is a great reminder to us as we seek to honor God in our business dealings.

Making a careless promise is no excuse to God and does not free us from obligation. Proverbs 20:25 says, "It is a trap for a man to dedicate something rashly and only later to consider his vows." May God give us all the wisdom we need to make smart decisions and honor Him in the way we deal with others.

Do you have an oath that has become hard to fulfill? Maybe you are making a decision right now that will be an obligation for you in the future. Ask God to guide you as you make tough decisions and remember to do everything as unto the Lord.

Niche of Rejection

By: Susanne Scheppmann

The rained dripped off the ends of the umbrella as I dashed to the community mailbox. I struggled to turn the key in the metal box, balance the umbrella, and hold my wiggly dog's leash as she strained to smell a nearby bush. Peering in the silver hole, I saw several catalogues and of course, the everyday pile of bills. Then I spied a letter with my letterhead and addressed to myself. Another rejection letter presented itself to me. Then my heart sank a notch lower. I could see two letters of rejection.

I trudged home in a spirit of defeat. Thinking to myself, *I probably have enough rejection letters to wallpaper at least half my house.* With a dour smile I continued, *Well, at least it would be something worthwhile to do with my writing.*

I closed the umbrella as my dog shook off the raindrops; she flung water up onto my stack of mail. Not even caring, I traipsed to my desk to open the dreaded letters.

As I sat down, I felt the Spirit of God remind me of his everlasting words, "For the sake of His great name the Lord will not reject his people, because the Lord was pleased to make you His own (1 Samuel 12:22). A comfort and peace settled over me. I realized that although some of my articles and books might not be accepted for publication, the Lord completely accepts my writing and me. I recalled B.J. Hoff's quote,

> *It matters not if the world has heard*
> *Or approves or understand*
> *The only applause we're meant to seek*
> *Is that of nail-scarred hands.*

I tried to remind myself, regardless of what others may say, I write for an audience of One, the Lord Jesus Christ.

I grabbed the thin opener, tore open the first envelope, and read the opening lines, "Although this proposed devotional would be a real encouragement, I am afraid I must decline it, since it is a niche market. It would be too targeted for our mass-market approach to publishing."

I began to smile, and then laugh. I had my own marketing niche: the niche of rejection. And was I ever successful at it!

As I reached for the next envelope, my heart felt a little lighter. Deep inside my heart, I knew I was pursuing a calling on my life. A part of this calling was to write with excellence. I looked up at my bulletin board. There, stuck to the cork, was a quote by Oswald Chambers on the topic of excellence:

> *Excellence is a difficult concept to communicate because it can be easily misread as neurotic perfectionism or snoot sophistication. But it is neither. On the contrary, it is the stuff of which greatness is made. It is the difference between just getting by and soaring—that which sets apart the significant from the superficial, the lasting from the temporary. Those who pursue it do so because of what pulsates within them, not because of what others say or do. Authentic excellence is not a performance. It is there whether anyone ever notices.*

Yes, even if no one ever notices I would be obedient to my call and the pursuit of excellence. Although, I might not ever get a book published, I am determined to write with increasing quality. I once heard someone say, "You can't make a talented man faithful, but God can make a faithful man talented." I want to be a *faithful and talented* woman in the hands of God.

I slid the silver letter opener under the edge of the next envelope expecting the same brief rejection paragraph. However, this rejection letter expressed a quiet encouragement to my writing soul. It was if the Lord smiled down and said, "See Susanne, you can do this!" It read, "This is a niche within the devotional category that we can only successfully publish a few titles over the course of several years. But I do want to encourage you to keep sharing this proposal with other houses. Please know the door here is always open to you if you would like to submit other book ideas. We like your style of writing."

Aha! Now that was a word for my weary writer's heart. I merrily reached down to pat my wet dog's head. My spirit, no longer dampened by rain or rejection, urged me back to my computer. With a renewed enthusiasm, I began to roll around in my mind the day's disheartening events: the rainy day, two rejection letters, and niche marketing warnings. However, the day also held a few glimmers of sunshine, the smell of rain, a frisky dog, and some encouraging words of support for my writing.

Although I could wallpaper my office with the eclectic niche of rejection correspondence that appears in my mailbox, I won't. Instead, I will continue to write for God.

> However, I consider my life worth nothing to me, if only I may finish the race and complete the task the Lord Jesus has given me—the task of testifying to the gospel of God's grace.
>
> —Acts 20:24

Susanne Scheppmann is an accomplished speaker and author. Published in several books and magazines, her heart's passion is for God's Word to become a living-daily part of everyone's life. A speaker for Proverbs 31 Ministries, Susanne speaks and writes to equip women to become godly in all areas of life. For more information, go to *www. proverbs31.org*.

Building On Rejection

Read I Corinthians 8:10-12, Hebrews 10:35-36

If you are like me, you have seen your share of rejection letters. There is nothing quite so disheartening as be-bopping out to the mailbox, only to find some form of rejection letter awaiting you. Talk about sucking the wind right out of your sails! Sometimes, it is enough to make you feel like quitting. I have actually quit before—several times, actually. I'm sure many of the authors represented in this book would also tell you they have quit before, too. Sometimes I have doubted God was calling me to this. Other times (and I am less proud of these moments) I have quit because I was frustrated and put out with God. "Fine!" I have told Him. "If you can't make this easier for me then I'm not going to do it!" And, yes, I'm certain I looked very much like a spoiled child when I said it. As Thelma Wells said in her interview, "I'm glad He doesn't fall off His throne when we act crazy."

I'm sure you would agree that Michael Jordan is probably the greatest basketball player ever. Not that I'm a huge basketball fan, but even I know that. What I didn't know until recently is that Michael Jordan was actually cut from his high school basketball team. This could have been a turning point for him. Quitting at that point probably seemed like the logical thing to do. After all, he wasn't good enough for the team, right? His coach had rejected him, right? He had failed.

But Michael Jordan didn't quit. He practiced faithfully all that year. He used rejection as an inspiration to work harder. And when it came time for the next tryouts, he was ready. The rest, as they say, is history. God doesn't want us to quit either. He wants us to persevere—to continue reaching for the prize no matter what setbacks come our way. Use your rejections as stepping stones toward better character and a stronger will to succeed. Then let God take care of the rest.

Don't throw away your rejection letters! I put mine in a notebook to keep. While they may be painful to look at now, someday they will be pleasant reminders of how far God has brought you.

Finding Purpose from Her Passion

An Interview with Ginger Plowman

Ginger Plowman has a passion for supporting and encouraging mothers. Years ago, her passion led her to start a moms' group at her church, which led to her leading a study of the book, *Shepherding A Child's Heart* by Tedd Tripp. As she used the book in her own home, she devised a chart for her children she called "Wise Words For Moms." The chart was essentially a personal way to practically apply the disciplining techniques she was learning through the book. When she showed her little chart to the other mothers in the group, they begged her to reproduce it. So, she took it to Kinko's® and made copies. Then she went one step further. She mailed Tedd Tripp a copy with a note enclosed, thanking him for writing his book and for the impact it had on her family. "I thought that would be the end of it," she says.

It turns out that Tedd Tripp had been getting requests for just such a chart from parents wherever he spoke. These parents wanted a practical tool to use in their homes as well. Tedd Tripp began selling Ginger's chart whenever he spoke, which was almost every weekend all over the country. On the inside cover, Ginger had listed a few of her speaking topics from seminars she had developed and her contact information. Before she knew it, she was receiving requests to speak from around the US. Her little chart was taking her places she had never dreamed.

It's important to note that, up to that point, Ginger had never considered herself a writer, though she felt comfortable speaking in front of crowds. She put together a seminar based on her chart called, *Reaching The Heart of Your Child.* After she had been giving her seminar for awhile, she realized that what Florence and Marita Littauer had said was true: "If you have something to speak about, you have something to write about." So, she decided to put her seminar into book form and present it to Tedd Tripp at an arranged meeting.

Remembering that first proposal, she laughs. "I knew nothing about writing a book! I basically had three *really* long chapters, based on the three sessions of my seminar. But Tedd was very good to give me some guidance and help me break the book into three sections of four chapters each, making it much more readable." That book, *Don't Make Me Count To Three,* was published by Tedd Tripp's Shepherd Press in 2004.

Through her journey from mom to speaker to writer, Ginger has seen God open some doors she would never have expected. Because of this, she has learned to look for God's leading in her life at all times. "I want to have my eyes open to which doors God is opening, while also realizing that sometimes He opens doors you aren't expecting," Ginger says. A recent example of that happening was when a group asked her to speak at a women's conference, but could not pay her full speaker's fee. After praying about it, Ginger felt led to come off her fee and do the conference anyway, rationalizing that it was a conference within driving distance, which would help.

As it turned out, the president of a major women's organization was at that conference. After sitting through her sessions, this man approached her and asked about her speaking at the organization's state conventions nationwide. One thing that Ginger has learned through experiences such as this is to be sensitive to the Spirit's leading and not get caught up in money or agendas. "My favorite things that happen to me are the things that I did not pursue in any way. That proves that God is orchestrating all of it."

As someone who writes on discipline, Ginger has occasionally found herself under fire for her views. This has also proved to be a valuable lesson and a chance for spiritual growth. "I have learned not to repay evil for evil, and to really ask God to show me if I was wrong. If I have inadvertently offended someone, I thank them for pointing it out to me and ask their forgiveness for discouraging them. I try to come back with a humble approach and to be others-oriented, as Christ was. Times like these have grown me as a writer."

Another way Ginger has grown as a writer is by learning to accept criticism. "It's really hard to hear anything negative when you feel that your work was ordained by God. It can really ruffle your feathers," she admits. She cites the example of her latest book, *Heaven At Home.* As she sat down with her publisher, Tedd Tripp, to go over the manuscript, she felt excited about her book. She sat back and waited for his words of praise.

Imagine her surprise when Tedd began to critique her book, especially her favorite chapter. "At that moment," she says, "I really didn't want to hear the truth in love; I wanted to hear 'How Great Thou Art'." As he began to talk, she willed herself to listen to what he had to say. She thought of Proverbs 27:6, "Wounds from a friend can be trusted, but an enemy multiplies kisses." She prayed, "Lord, if there is something to what he is saying, then please let me hear it. If re-writing some of this book will bring more glory to You, then change my heart." Ultimately, Tedd's words helped her to improve the book and make it more glorifying to Christ. Ginger tossed out the chapter she loved, and re-wrote it completely. She ended up with a chapter that was so much better than the original, and is now thankful for this valuable lesson in accepting and implementing criticism in her writing.

As Ginger has begun speaking more and more, she has become familiar with the fun parts of writing and speaking, and the not-so-fun parts. She shared this e-mail with several friends, and has given permission for it to be printed here:

Boy did I have a crap day. We do not say "crap" in our home, but somehow, it's the only appropriate word for this day. I flew to Ohio to speak at a women's banquet last night. I was tired and just really didn't want to be there. You know how some days you're "on" and some days you're not? It was one of those "not" days. I am assuming God used it in spite of how I felt. I had several ladies hug me in tears afterwards and explain how God used it in their lives, but I was thinking, "I can't believe God used it at all!"

I had scheduled my return flight so that I would be home by lunch today. So I got up early and arrived at the airport two hours ahead of schedule only to find that the flight had been canceled and the next one wouldn't leave for five hours. That's SEVEN hours in the airport. THEN I was placed in the back of the plane (I hate that) beside an obnoxious, spoiled five-year-old and his mom-servant who obviously hasn't read my book. THEN, when I arrived back in Atlanta the luggage was delayed by an hour for reasons that made no sense to me. THEN, I yanked my fake fingernail (cemented to my real fingernail) half way off the nail bed trying to lift my eighty-five pound suitcase (full of unsold products) off the baggage carousel. THEN, ten steps prior to walking through the exit door that led to my car it started pouring down rain. By the time I made it to the car my finger was throbbing, black streaks of mascara were running down my face, and I looked like a drowned rat. Oh the glamorous life of a speaker!

Not only does Ginger have a great sense of humor, but she is also a "master at marketing." She has graciously shared a few of her marketing ideas below:

- Get Sally Stuart's *Christian Writers Market Guide*. Look up publishers who might be interested in your book. This guide tells what each publisher is looking for and WHO to contact. Don't send a proposal that is addressed generically. Send it to the right person's attention. Call that person before sending it and have a well thought out 45-second verbal pitch saying what your book is about and why it's needed in today's market. Don't talk too long. Write out what you want to say so that it's well worded and conveys exactly what you want in 45-60 seconds.

- Go to writers' conferences where you'll have opportunities to meet face to face with publishers. Know what you will say! Again, I recommend pre-thinking your verbal pitch, as this will make you more confident in your project. Have your proposal ready. (See Appendix A: How To Write A Book Proposal.)

- When promoting your book: Know who the audience is and seek opportunities to speak to that particular audience. If it's on motherhood, homemaking, etc. look into MOPS groups. If it's on women's topics, send a flier with a picture of book and your availability to speak on your topic to women's coordinators at local (or national if you're interested in traveling) churches. Contact companies that might be interested in carrying your book. Offer to do book signings at Books-A-Million, Barnes and Noble, etc—they will carry your book when you do book signings for them. Look into annual conferences where workshops are offered and lead a workshop on the subject of your book . . . of course, your book will be available for purchase.

- Attend the National Religious Broadcasters convention (www.nrb.org) and give a packet of information to radio and TV producers. Your packet should include a personalized letter, your bio, suggested interview questions, and your book. If you can't afford to give books away, include a nice one-page flyer with the cover, description, and your contact info. In the cover letter say that if they are interested in doing an interview with you, that you will gladly send them a copy of the book at their request. Be sure to get their business cards so that you can follow up with a phone call after a month or so.

- If you can't attend NRB, do internet searches for Christian radio and TV contacts. Call them, introduce yourself and tell them what you offer as far as an interview. Be excited and enthusiastic. Think through what you will say before you call. I recommend writing it down so you sound more professional and don't stumble over your words. Practice what you will say so that it doesn't sound as though you are reading it. Offer to send them a packet of information about you.

Ginger has embarked on an amazing adventure with God, taking her places she would never have imagined and sometimes growing her in ways she never would have chosen. As she looks towards the future of her writing career, she knows that triumphs, successes, and blessings are coupled with trials, rejections, and heart-breaking disappointments. However, by utilizing her talents for the glory of God, she also knows that every rejection and every disappointment are filtered through God's hand and always lead to His higher purpose. Ginger concludes, "As long as I am seeking God's will as a writer, I know He will use me to point others to Jesus and glorify His name . . . and that's what it's all about!"

Ginger Plowman, author of *Don't Make Me Count to Three,* is the founder of Preparing the Way Ministries for which she speaks at women's events and parenting conferences across the country. Visit her web site at *www.gingerplowman.com.*

Writing The Vision

Read Habakkuk 2:2-3

It began with a passion in your life. Maybe your passion is for abused women, unwed mothers, single parents or the homeless. Maybe your heart goes out to the young mothers you see struggling in the grocery store. Maybe you simply have a passion to reach the lost, no matter where they are. Whatever your passion is, it is what drives you into action. This action is your passion in motion, your dream being lived out. You have a story to share and people to minister to. Steadily, cautiously, you stepped out, trusting God to move in a mighty way. You started to see a difference. You were making an impact. Your dream became a vision and you were able to see it lived out.

In this passage, we are instructed to write down the vision God has given to us, so that those who read it may run with it. I have a friend who feels called to adopt internationally. God has moved in miraculous ways to confirm that He has, indeed, called their family to this. This passage has inspired her to write down all that God has shown her so that someday her story will hopefully inspire others to also adopt internationally. She knows that if she does not keep a written record, she will simply forget and the power in her story will be lost. On days when she questions whether she will ever hold this child in her arms, she clings to verse three: "Though it linger, wait for it; it will certainly come and will not delay." From passion, to dream, to vision—we can all write down our revelations from God so that we may encourage others to take action through our story.

As you journey through the publishing maze, keep a journal of what God is showing you. Don't get so focused on the process that you forget about preserving the lessons He is teaching you along the way.

Yeah, Right!

• •

By: Rachael Carman

How did I get into speaking and writing? What did I do? Who did I talk to? When did it all start? Boy, good questions. And I thought that I knew the answers. That was until I tried to write this article. When my friend called me and asked me to do this, I said, "Sure. No problem. 1300 words? Walk in the park." After all, I just turned in 52,000 to my editor. I think that I can come up with 1300. "A couple of weeks, you got it." Yeah, right.

Well, let me start by saying that I went way over the original deadline. It seems I had underestimated the difficulty of this task. I think that I have about 15 different starts to this article. Let's see, there is the dramatic recounting of the day I received the message from Focus on the Family. Then there is the recounting of all of the events that led up to the call, a kind of "the rest of the story" approach. I also tried starting the article describing a familiar cartoon scene from my childhood. It did not work out very well.

In short I think that I have close to 5,000 words down now and I still do not have anything comprehensible. Why is that? It's because so many details of my life won't fit into the set word limit for this article. See, when I start to tell my story, every specific aspect matters. Every particular person, situation, and circumstance matters. God, the master craftsman, weaves them together to make the tapestry.

For example, it matters that my dad is a preacher and an excellent writer. It matters that I have always aspired to writing, but have struggled with spelling and been liberated by spell check! It is important that I have been encouraged by audience members, friends and family to pursue my writing. And it matters that I have seven children. These and literally hundreds of other elements of my life make up the whole picture and answer all of the questions.

In short, my pursuing a publisher was about a six-year journey. It started with attending a CLASS Seminar and culminated with a contract with Focus on the Family. It included a few articles along the way in *Proverbs 31 Magazine,* advice and encouragement from Lysa TerKeurst, and two appointments with Focus on the Family through the Proverbs 31 She Speaks Seminar. But even with all of that, it did not happen like I thought it would or when I thought it would.

When I got the call from Focus on the Family that they wanted to publish my proposed book, all I could do was laugh. Yeah, right, I thought. See, by the time I got their message. (Yes, did you catch that? I even missed the call. They left me a message.) I was not thinking about the book. So much had happened since the time I had met with Mark Maddox. We had sold our house, packed everything up, put half of it in storage, moved into a rental, and I had given birth to our seventh child. Honestly, although I prayed regularly for the book and the future of my ministry, I was not obsessing.

Throughout my first two attempts to publish, a book contract was all I could think about. And I didn't just think about it, I meditated on it, focused on it. In truth, I couldn't think of much else. Every day when I walked out to the mailbox I would wonder if this might be the day. And day after day I was disappointed. When the letters did finally come, they were not the ones I had desired. My deep disappointment surprised me and served as a wake-up call back to the things and thoughts that really mattered.

By the third time I proposed the book, I was much more relaxed. I had learned a thing or two. And what I learned is more important than the fact that I got the call. In the interim between the second rejection and the third proposal, I realized that my getting published was not up to these editors, it was up to God. Sadly, I had forgotten this important fact. I had gotten caught up in the meetings and the names and the impressions. Through my prayer times God began speaking to my heart and reminding me that if He wanted me published, He would get me published. And secondly, I learned that although the message He had given me was fresh and insightful, in the end it was still His message, not mine. There had been a couple of times when I had given way to panic, what if someone else proposed the same unique idea and they got published instead of me? This is my book! But God taught me that it was never mine in its origination, only it in its presentation.

All of this to say that by the time I got the message from Focus, I had really and finally left it up to God. So much so that I could pray about it and leave it at the Throne of Grace. Another thing that occurred during this period was a humbling process. I began to think that maybe I didn't have anything to say after all. I was relearning that I still had so much to learn myself, still so many rough edges. This was, of course, exactly where God wanted me to be so that I would know and experience Him as I wrote the book.

By the time Focus on the Family wanted to publish the book, I knew that He was going to have to write the book through me. We were living in a rental house while our new one was due to be started, I had a six week old baby and was homeschooling his six older siblings. I felt like I was in the middle of a desert, also known as the postpartum fog—those six weeks after giving birth when I am getting no sleep and there are too many hormones coursing through my veins. I have learned that I should not make any important decisions during this time, much less any commitments. *This is where you want me to write, here where I feel so empty, where I feel so out of sorts, here where I feel so uninspired and so overwhelmed? Here? Now? Yeah, right.* Of course, it WAS the right time because it was His time. I was humbled, anxious and excited all at the same time.

There were two Bible verses that echoed in my head throughout the writing project. The first was John 3:30 where John the Baptist said, "I must become less and He must become greater." It has been my prayer that this book will draw its readers into a more intimate relationship with God. I want them to want more of Him. And the second verse was John 15:5 where Jesus said, "Apart from me you can do nothing." I lived this verse! There were times when I sat down to write, but came up dry because I was trying to do it of myself. There were other times when I started out my writing time at the foot of His throne, seeking Him and He poured forth "beyond what I could ask or imagine." It was a divine and providential appointment, an opportunity for me to let His message flow through me for His glory.

The last year has been a whirlwind of peace. I cannot explain to you all that He has done, except to say that He has done it all and more. He has walked me through one of the busiest times with all of its confusion and frustrations, all of its joy and anticipation. He held my hand and held me up as I, by His strength, chose again and again against doubt, fear, defeat, and frustration. Time and time again I was tempted to waiver and shrink from the tasks set before me, but "He is my Rock and my Salvation, In Him will I trust." You can trust Him too. Do your circumstances seem impossible? Does what He has called you to do seem overwhelming? Do you think that He has forgotten you? Do you wonder if He will ever give you an outlet for all you have learned about Him and His faithfulness? Do you long to encourage others? "Seek first His kingdom and all of these things will be added to you."

Rachael Carman is the wife of Davis and homeschooling mother of seven children. She leads a yearly retreat for homeschool moms called "Real Refreshment." Her ministry web site is *www.rdcministries.org*. She is the author of *Sound Bites From Heaven: What God Wants Us To Hear When We Talk To Our Kids*, due to be released by Focus on the Family in September of 2005.

The Right Order

Read Psalm 37:4-5, Psalm 16: 5-8, Job 22:21-29

Many of us know Psalm 37:4 by heart. We can quote it reflexively and honestly desire to fulfill what it says. But do we have the verse in the right order? As Kendra Smiley points out, many of us get this verse backwards. We read the part about getting the desires of our heart and say, "That's what I want!" We figure out how we can delight ourselves in the Lord *because* we want the desires of our heart. The verse goes in proper order: first, we delight ourselves in the Lord through no motive except to develop a love relationship, a dependency on Him as our Abba Father. As this relationship deepens and our connection to Him grows stronger, our desires—the desire of our hearts—match His. Kendra says, "We know His desire for our hearts because we are so close." Our selfish human agendas are removed when the proper order is in place.

Psalm 37:5 goes on to say, "Commit your way to the Lord." Proverbs 16:3 tells us to, "Commit to the Lord whatever you do and your plans will succeed." Here again, we get it backward. We read that verse and say, "Well, I want my plans to succeed so I better commit them to the Lord." In our limited language, we think to "commit" means to tell Him our plans before we do it so He can go ahead and bless them. In reality, this word literally means "to roll." We are to roll our burdens onto Him, to climb up into His lap and tell Him our troubles and our worries. While they may be a burden to us, they are never too much for Him. I Peter 5:7 says, "Cast all your anxiety on Him because He cares for you." As in any love relationship, what matters to you matters to Him.

Do you have big plans for your writing? Are you dreaming about seeing your name on the cover of a book? Maybe there's a conference you'd like to speak at and you're petitioning the Lord to make it happen for you. Don't get the verse in the wrong order. Spend time with the Lord. Make Him your heart's desire and let Him take care of the rest. As Kendra says, "Getting it in the right order is so awesome."

Look up the word "delight" in a Bible concordance. Spend time learning what God has to say about delighting yourself in Him.

*Special thanks to Kendra Smiley, whose words to me inspired this devotional.

A Heart for Home and Him

An Interview with Jill Savage

Jill Savage never aspired to be a writer and a speaker. She was a pastor's wife and mother of four when she began looking for mothers who were just a few steps ahead of her for guidance. "I was struggling," she recalls. She went to her growing moms' group at church and proposed the idea for a conference for stay-at-home moms. "We held our first conference and expected 400 women. We had 1100. The next year we had 2800 women. We realized we had stumbled onto a real need for women. So really, Hearts at Home was born out of my own needs as a mom."

Because of her position as founder, Jill found herself writing articles for the Hearts at Home newsletter. "My goal was, and is, to help moms feel normal, to deal with real struggles and real emotions and to cast a vision as to why what we are doing is important." With the success of the conferences, their city's newspaper asked her to write a column with three other writers on family and motherhood. Writing the column once a month became Jill's first official writing job.

As Hearts at Home grew and expanded their conferences into other cities, publishers began coming to them with offers. "We needed another vehicle to take our message beyond the conferences," Jill explains. "We were in a unique position in that publishers were knocking on our door instead of the other way around." Jill met with a mentor from another ministry that was about five steps ahead of Hearts to get advice about publishing. The woman advised her to get an agent and let the agent talk to publishers to make the right connection.

The ministry did find an agent that valued their work to lead them through the publishing process. "We did not know what we were doing," Jill remembers. Her experience with their agent has made her a firm believer in agents. "That was the best advice I could have gotten," she says. "Agents know the industry and we don't, at least, not like they do." From a financial standpoint, Jill has found that agents pay for themselves. "A good agent," she says, "Should cost you nothing because you will get a better contract."

Jill remembers her first book as an eye-opening experience. Because of her experience with writing countless articles for Hearts at Home, she had become quite efficient at taking most any concept and developing it into a 700 to 1000 word article. "Well, 700 to 1000 words is like the first two pages of one chapter!" she says. "It was overwhelming and intimidating," she remembers.

After she submitted her manuscript, she got it back for editing. "I had always been a strong writer," she says. "So, it was very humbling to see all those red marks all over it." One problem for Jill was that she did not receive adequate information for new authors. Through a miscommunication, she never received her new author packet just to answer some basic questions. "I was doing it blindly because of that," she says. In the end, she discovered that she was short by five chapters. In spite of the panic she initially felt at hearing that news, she created what ultimately became the most popular part of the book. Remembering that time she says, "I was just learning the ropes."

That valuable first experience, combined with Hearts' own publishing division, has led to Jill being in a position to give good solid advice to writers. She offers these ten tips:

1. Regardless of whether you ever get published or not, one of the things you need to grab hold of is that publishing does not validate your story.
2. Start out by writing articles. Write for small magazines or your church newsletter. The internet is a great resource to place articles. You can even post articles on your own web site. The point is to develop your skills.
3. Just because you want to write doesn't mean you can write. Learn to take constructive criticism.
4. Go to writers' conferences. Jill recommends Write To Publish, Speak Up, and CLASS.
5. If you have a book on your heart that you want to find a publisher for, do not just write the book. Prepare a proposal first. By writing the book, you are saying that you are unwilling to have the publisher's input and that you have it all figured out already. It is difficult for a publisher to match up their needs with something that has already been decided.
6. If you want to self-publish, then go ahead and write the whole book, just make sure that you have a good editor.

7. Sometimes a really strong proposal just doesn't fit a publisher's basic needs. That doesn't mean it's not a strong book. Publishers are generally looking for a specific message and voice. In that respect, rejection can come in all forms.

8. Get a good agent. Be wary of agents that charge more than 15% or that charge up front costs just to look at your work. If you have trouble finding an agent, get some honest feedback from the ones who won't represent you so that you can improve.

9. Find ways to speak on whatever your passion is. This becomes your platform. If you are really called to write and speak on this topic, you usually won't be able to stop talking about it. Look for small arenas to speak in at first—your church, community groups, etc. Don't speak for pay, speak for experience. Jill did not get paid to speak for the first ten years she spoke.

10. Make sure you have the support of your family. Really evaluate the season of life you are in before you take on too much. Establish good communication with your spouse about the whole process.

Jill has experienced her own stretching as her family adjusted to her increasing demands as author and speaker. "I could have never done what I'm doing now when my children were preschoolers," she explains. "Now that they are in school, I have established daytime hours to write. I have boundaries in place so that I am done when they get home from school. I'm not pulled in one-hundred different directions. Not to say that we don't eat lots of frozen pizza when I'm on deadline!" she laughs.

Deadlines were a bit of an initial communication struggle for her and her husband. "I think it took us to about the third book to negotiate deadlines," she laughs. "When I would turn in a manuscript, he would think it was done, but then it would come back and I would have a new deadline for edits. In his mind, I was done, but I knew I was only done for a season. I had a clear picture of what the whole journey looked like, but he didn't. I had to do a better job communicating the bigger picture and he had to learn to educate himself by asking questions about the process."

Jill makes all her business decisions based on her marriage and family. "I turn down more speaking engagements than I take," she says. "I have to preserve the integrity of my message by truly being a mother at home. I have to do laundry, make dinner, and clean my house like all stay-at-home moms."

Though she never aspired to be a writer or a speaker, Jill juggles her roles with efficiency and grace, daily relying on God to keep her perspectives in place. "I fought against this role for a long time," she says. "Because I didn't aspire to this, it took awhile to sink in that God did call me to it. My life is greatly enriched by the people I meet and the stories I hear. It can be exhausting, but I know I'm blessed."

Jill Savage (*www.jillsavage.org*) is a pastor's wife and mother of five. She serves as the Executive Director of Hearts at Home (www.hearts-at-home.org), an organization designed to encourage women in the profession of motherhood. Jill is the author of four books including *Professionalizing Motherhood* and *Is There Really Sex After Kids?* Jill lives with her family in Normal, Illinois.

Priorities In Place

Read I Samuel 2:12, 17, 22-24, 3:13, 8:1-5

I heard a story once about a woman in ministry who had a dream one night. In her dream, the Lord came to her and took her up on a hill overlooking a valley. Standing in the valley were the thousands of people who had come to know the Lord through her ministry. As she stood there beside the Lord, surveying all the people, she thought, "It doesn't get any better than this." She looked over at the Lord and tried to imagine what He was thinking. Eagerly, she waited for Him to lavish her with praise for a job well done. Imagine her surprise when He extended His hand, gesturing to the mass of people below and asked her, "Where are your children?"

The scripture today gives different accounts of people in ministry who did amazing things for God, but failed their own children. In both accounts, these men had to hear about what their children were doing from other people. Clearly they were not with their family enough to know what was going on firsthand. Their children's lack of character was a direct reflection on them. God knew that they had allowed their position of ministry to detract from their task of raising and disciplining their children, and He held them accountable for it. God was dishonored when these men were too involved in ministry to watch over their family's spiritual growth.

There is a powerful lesson in these two examples and the example of the woman's dream. While ministry is a calling from God and an excellent way to use our gifts and talents, it is not meant to take away from the needs of our family. We must remember that discipling our children and meeting our husband's needs is of the utmost importance to God. We can't afford to make the mistake of getting our priorities out of order. A decision to neglect our responsibilities will most certainly have eternal ramifications.

Ask God to show you if your ministry is taking you away from your obligation to your family. Don't allow money or pride or big dreams to deter you from ministering to the people God placed in your life first. If this is an area you struggle with, set up some accountability with a trusted friend who won't be afraid to call you on the carpet when you need your priorities adjusted.

One Mother's Mission
• •

By: Karen Ehman

"Karen is a terrific poet. She'll be an author someday." "You have a flair for creative writing. Keep it up!" "Boy . . . can that girl talk! Hopefully someday she'll get paid to do it!"

Brief remarks on a report card, casual comments spoken aloud. These phrases echoed in the mind of this then junior-high-aged girl as I secretly longed for them to come true. Were they right? Me? An author or speaker? I certainly hoped they were. However, God had much to teach me much about *His* plans for my desires.

By high school, I attempted small projects—writing minutes for Student Council meetings, introducing the speaker at the Junior-Senior Banquet. I eventually landed a position reporting for the school newspaper in high school as well as at my small Christian college. It was then I tried my hand at vocal performance and acting, both of which I loved! Once married, I settled into my life, ready to be a stay-at-home wife and mother but wondering how I could still pursue my now less-secret passions for performance, writing and speaking.

I soon became part of a group of four women who provided music and drama for mother-daughter banquets and women's events. Primarily a local ministry, it was also such fun! After my first child was born, I planned to continue this ministry, hoping to see it expand. I was not prepared, however, for the darling-yet-colicky-wouldn't-take-a-bottle-even-of-breast-milk-baby that was to be my daughter! Mother and child being apart for more than two hours at a stretch? It just wasn't going to happen. What ensued in the next few years was a stripping away of my identity—an identity that was rooted in what I did or how I performed, not in my position in Christ. Sadly, I cared far more about who others thought I was, rather than who God was calling me to be.

I felt my identity was gone. I was known only as "the youth pastor's wife" or "so-and-so's mom". My days were spent wiping and rocking; cooking and cleaning. Even though I loved my family, I also quietly resented them, feeling that my life as an at-home mom was keeping me from my dreams.

Finally I came to a point of willful surrender. Deciding that it was the only option, I told God I'd be content to be known as a "Mrs." and a "mom" but He would need to take away my desire to perform, speak and write. Just as He often does, God whispered a plan to my heart that I had not thought of. He nudged me to begin using my talents to bless my family instead of to make my name known. I was convicted of my wrong motives and purposed in my heart that I would use my gifts to love and serve my family first (and perhaps only).

What happened next was nothing short of miraculous for this otter-personality-type, stage-loving-gal. I became content to sing lullabies and silly songs with my children as my only audience. I began to use my imaginative mind and love for drama to act out exciting Bible stories or to invent different voices for the characters in the books we read aloud at bedtime. I threw myself into writing love letters to my husband, clever poems for my kids and simple musings to myself. I honestly felt that outside ministry opportunities would never come my way and I was surprisingly okay with it!

One sunny spring afternoon I received a phone call from my friend Bonnie. She and her husband were entering full-time ministry, forcing her to discontinue the newsletter she had started for stay-at-home moms unless she could find someone to take it over. While praying for such a person, God turned her thoughts to me. Knowing I'd get the go-ahead from Todd, I blurted out "Yes!" before she even had a chance to finish posing her question, although I neither owned a computer nor knew how to operate one! I would edit the reader-written newsletter four times a year and also write a column each issue. The rest of the publication was chock-full of ideas that would encourage full-time moms serving Christ at home. I happily served as editor of *A Mother's Mission Newsletter* for the next five years and through two more babies!

Doors opened. I began to speak at area moms groups and soon stumbled upon a national ministry for mothers called *Hearts at Home*. While attending my first conference, during a workshop a staff volunteer introduced the speaker. My heart skipped a beat as I thought to myself: "Oh to be the woman up there . . . *who gets to introduce the speaker!*" Little did I know that God would give me the opportunity and His permission not only to be a workshop speaker myself, but to perform drama and speak from the main stage to over 10,000 women annually.

I now do free-lance work for a few magazines, serve as project creator for the *Hearts at Home Mom's Planner,* an organizational tool that helps mothers organize their personal, family and devotional life and have even co-authored two books! My friend Kelly and I led a workshop in 1998 on creative and cost-effective gifts that moms and kids can make. Three years later my friend Trish joined us as we self-published a book entitled *Homespun Gifts From the Heart* based on that talk. The book was well received by the many ladies who heard us speak. We sent a copy of the book along with a cover letter explaining how God was using this work by three unknown Michigan moms to four different publishers. Within twenty-four hours we received an e-mail response from an editor at Baker Publishing Group. A contract was signed and nine months later God gave birth to our first published book! It received national attention as I was honored to be a guest on Dr. James Dobson's Focus on the Family broadcast and we appeared on several national radio and television shows as well. This led to a second book. *Homespun Memories for the Heart* is a tool for moms who long to celebrate holidays, holy days and the everyday in such a way as to make lasting memories.

Now rather than trying to tuck my family in around the edges of my life, our entire family has found a ministry! I write early in the morning or late at night and my clan often accompanies me to speaking engagements. This way they can keep me humble as they work at my book table. When someone asks me to sign a book, they are nearby, ready to chime in . . . *"Don't forget to write that sometimes you holler at your kids!"*

The most wonderful aspect of this journey has been the clear affirmation I have received from God. He created me with a bent, one that was evident even as a grade school girl growing up in the Midwest. He fashioned me with gifts that He intended for me to use for HIS glory—not for mine. My creator gave me passions, but showed me that they didn't have to be pursued at the expense of my family. He opened up avenues for me to pursue those passions while using them to encourage women in their roles as godly wives and mothers.

What about you? Are there voices from your past reminding you of a hidden ability to write or speak? Listen to them but pray that God will show you *His* will and *His* way. Ask Him to open doors for you so that you need only to walk obediently through. You can pursue your passions without sacrificing your most important ministry—the one that includes the often mundane, yet always holy, duties of marriage and motherhood.

Karen Ehman is a graduate of Spring Arbor University, the wife of Todd and the home-schooling mother of three. She is a speaker, a free-lance writer, the co-author of two books and creator of the *Hearts at Home Mom's Planner.* She has been a guest on national television and radio programs including *At Home Live, The Harvest Show, Moody Midday Connection* and Dr. James Dobson's *Focus on the Family*.

For I know the plans I have for you," declares the LORD, "plans to prosper you and not to harm you, plans to give you hope and a future."

—Jeremiah 29:11

Reaching Hearts

Read Jeremiah 24:7, Luke 6:4-5

If you have given your heart to the Lord, how much of it have you given to Him? In the verse in Jeremiah, God says that He wants all of our heart. We should hold nothing back in our commitment to Him.

If you have a desire to write and to share Him with others, then He has clearly given you a heart to know Him as the verse says. The more you learn, the more you have to share. And yet, knowing Him on an intellectual level and loving Him with all your heart are two different things.

As the verse in Luke tells us, what we know in our heads is not nearly as effective as communicating what we know in our hearts. Theological head knowledge may serve you well in a seminary class, but it isn't going to change lives and win souls like a simple story told from the heart. I Corinthians 13:1 says, "If I speak in the tongues of angels, but have not love, I am only a resounding gong or a clanging symbol." The key to reaching hearts is committing our own hearts fully to God.

A friend of mine recently shared how her husband had really struggled to connect with the men in their church. "The trouble is," my friend said, "All of the men in our church know the Bible really well. Though they don't mean to, they make my husband feel stupid. He tried the men's Bible study but he struggled because they would get off on long theological debates he could not participate in, and wasn't interested in." And then my friend said something that really struck me: "All he wanted was someone to talk to, to connect with and share his struggles with." My friend's husband ultimately quit the Bible study and has slipped further away from the church. Instead of reaching his heart, the men intimidated him and lost him all together.

As we seek to share Christ and communicate His truths, may we constantly speak from our hearts to the hearts of those who need Him and may God help us to find a way to show His love in everything we say and do.

Think of a time when you have been around someone who is a spiritual giant to you. Did that person make you feel intimidated or loved? How did they do that? Write down some of their attitudes and actions and purpose to either imitate or improve upon their example.

*Creating Faith-
Infused Fiction*

• •

An Interview with Allen Arnold

As senior Vice President and publisher for Thomas Nelson's fiction division, Westbow Press, Allen Arnold sees hundreds of manuscripts cross his desk each year, yet he only signs about two new writers per year. Allen says, "When you take the numbers of new writers hoping to get their first novel published, and then add to that the number of proven authors pitching new ideas, you can see the challenge that faces new authors. It's hard to get your foot in the door."

Allen suggests three steps that will give new writers a competitive edge in the publishing world:

1. Join a writing critique group. Don't solely rely on your mom and sister's opinion of your writing. Seek sincere, knowledgeable feedback from trusted sources. Allen suggests searching the internet for writers' groups in your area, saying that "Any mid-size community should have something to offer. If not, start your own writers' group."

2. If you have polished your work and are ready to take the next step, you should secure an agent. In his position, Allen has come to value the role agents play because they serve as a pre-screening of sorts, and cut through the clutter.

3. Finally, if you have trouble securing an agent, realize that this may mean that your novel just isn't ready to show to a publisher. While you can consider testing the market by self-publishing, that is an expensive and risky option. But, it can pay big dividends if you feel confident that your novel is ready for the world to see. If that's the case, instead of waiting for publishers to take notice, show them what you can

do with the book. Allen cites bestsellers like *The Christmas Box* by Richard Paul Evans and *Eragon* by Christopher Paolini as examples of fiction books which were self published prior to being picked up by a bigger publishing house. Both of these books went on to huge success, largely due to the authors' initial belief in their project.

Allen stresses that all writers should take these steps. "If you don't, it decreases your odds tremendously. If you do, it puts you head and shoulders above the competition." Additionally, Allen looks for a well-honed proposal including the first three chapters of the book. Few editors have time to wade through a 500-page manuscript. "If you're a good acquisitions editor, you can tell if they have what it takes in just a few chapters." As for writing style, he looks for fiction that is not preachy. "To me, if you want to preach a sermon, write nonfiction. Don't use cardboard characters and a nonexistent plot just to further your message. If you take away your message, do you still have a story? That's what we're looking for—great stories told from a Christian worldview."

Allen has always been an avid reader and fan of fiction. Prior to publishing, he worked in advertising agencies. In 1992, he joined Word Publishing (now Thomas Nelson) in their marketing department. In 2003, he launched Westbow Press, the company's new fiction division. He has found that his background in marketing and packaging has been a good fit with publishing and acquisitions.

In his role at Westbow Press, Allen is passionate about creating great works of Christian fiction. Though he feels that Christian fiction has gotten better in the last five years, there is still room to grow. He stresses the need for writers to trust their reader to think without spoon-feeding them. "That can be degrading for the reader—and it doesn't make for a very entertaining read," he adds.

Westbow Press is Allen's effort to produce God-honoring products that are entertaining and culturally relevant. "We want to create mainstream awareness from a Christian worldview," he says. "We don't seek to evangelize evangelicals."

Thomas Nelson is one of the ten largest publishers in the world. For this reason, they do not get caught up in whether a book "crosses over" into the secular marketplace. "When you start with a great story, the novel doesn't have to cross over anything. It will appeal to both CBA and general market readers." Allen deems this as merely semantics. "We have set channels we market through. We don't have special marketing just for Christian projects. Our goal is to publish so that someone who has never darkened the door of a church can find these products and be impacted by them. That doesn't mean that the character must get saved at the end and go riding off into the sunset for the book to make its mark."

Allen calls Westbow Press' fiction "faith-infused fiction." He draws a great analogy of a beautiful landscape painted by a Christian painter. The artist does not feel compelled to place a cross somewhere in the landscape just to emphasize his faith. And yet, the beauty of God's creation and the artist's appreciation of the Creator is still evident to everyone that encounters that painting. The same is true of fiction. It is more than possible to produce great fiction from a Christian worldview—in fact that is how great literature has been done for centuries. Allen gives the example of early classics written by those who saw the world from a Christian worldview.

Most of all, Allen points out that fiction is a valuable teaching tool. "Christ told parables," he says, "But He didn't explain them all. He trusted the people to learn from His teachings, which is what any good writer should do."

Allen Arnold is Publisher and Senior Vice President of WestBow Press, the fiction division of Thomas Nelson Publishers. As Publisher of WestBow, Arnold's goal is to deliver the best stories to the broadest possible audience in the most entertaining, relevant, and God-honoring way possible. A veteran of the publishing industry since 1992, he's overseen the marketing and branding of many best-selling Christian authors including Max Lucado, Ted Dekker, John Eldredge, and Frank Peretti. Prior to that, Arnold promoted some of the top consumer brands while working with some of the country's leading agencies—including Ogilvy & Mather and The Richards Group. His favorite way to spend the day is with his wife and two young children—preferably with a C.S. Lewis book close at hand as well!

The Power of Stories

Read Matthew 13:10-17, 34-35, Mark 4: 11-12, 33-34

In our last devotional, we talked about how sharing simple stories from the heart can be very effective in reaching people. In the scriptures today, we see Jesus doing just that whenever He stood before crowds. Unlike the Pharisees, who stood in public praying aloud and spouting scripture (Matthew 15:9), Jesus gave easily applicable illustrations to the crowd based on everyday things they would understand. Put simply, He was a master storyteller.

If you think back through some of His parables, He rarely mentioned God directly. And yet, His stories simply and effectively pointed the people towards God. He made them see God in everything they encountered. Because of this, He became a God who was near—not the far-off God the Pharisees were always preaching about. Jesus' stories put God within the people's grasp.

At that point, the people had a choice to make: to remain in the dark or to follow Jesus, the light. We see in the scriptures for today that Jesus did not explain the parables to the people. The parables were meant to test their responsiveness. Later, when He was alone with His disciples, He explained the meaning. His disciples were ready for more information, but He knew the others needed time to process what they had heard. Jesus did not expect instant transformation. The average distance from the head to the heart is 18 inches. Though that may seem like a short distance, sometimes that 18 inches can be a long journey indeed. Jesus knew that it takes time to reach the hearts of people.

When we write or speak, we should rely on Jesus' perfect example. It is too easy to fall into the role of "authority", when what people really want is a friend. We can share our humble illustrations and life experiences, and let God expand our little offering to bless the lives of many.

Has God brought a life illustration to mind recently that you should share with others? Ask Him to keep your eyes and ears open to anything that would best reflect Him and make Him more real to the world.

An Editor's Perspective

. . . .

An Interview with Denny Boultinghouse

Denny Boultinghouse did not start out in Christian publishing—he started out in Christian ministry. After serving as a minister in a church for ten years, he became an editor for a Christian publication. From there, the Lord opened doors that led him to his current position as Executive Editor for Howard Publishing Company. Denny describes himself as an avid reader and book buyer on a variety of subjects. Denny has now been in Christian publishing for twenty years.

Recently, he has seen publishers tightening their belts by cutting back on the number of new titles released each year. He explains that publishers must spend between $20,000 to $30,000 on a book before it is ever published, making any project an expensive and risky process. The fact that publishers have had to cut back on the number of titles they do makes it much more difficult to get published. Denny also notes that more publishers are going towards not accepting unsolicited manuscripts, except at writers' conferences and through literary agents.

Denny is quick to point out that writers need to understand that Christian publishing is a business and not a ministry. When a publisher is deciding whether to publish a book, they run a profit and loss statement (called a P&L) on that book. If they know that they can realistically sell 3000 copies but need to sell 9000 to break even, then they can not do that project. "Otherwise," he says, "We would end up with a warehouse full of books we can't sell." For this reason, Denny strongly advises that writers familiarize themselves with the process of publishing. Most of all, though, he emphasizes that if you feel a calling to write, you should never let the numbers discourage you.

As an acquisitions editor, he looks for books that are well done, have a message, and have a "hook" to draw the reader in. For him, the first essential a writer must have is a strong query or proposal. He encourages writers to invest in books on writing proposals to learn how to put one together, such as Jeff Herman's *Write The Perfect Book Proposal*. (Also see "Appendix A: How To Write A Proposal")

One additional point Denny makes to potential authors involves the query or proposal letter. He says, "Do not waste a paragraph of your letter telling the editorial team how the Holy Spirit told you to write this book or that you want to bless people with your writing. That assumption is already understood. Instead, use your proposal letter to show the publisher something different about what you are offering. Point out your catchy title and your effective storytelling."

Denny also looks for a great title. He uses a Christian leadership book that Howard published called *They Smell Like Sheep* as an example. This book attracted attention because of its catchy title, which served as a hook. Even though the author was an unknown to consumers, readers still wanted to pick up this book to find out more, simply because of its unique title. Even with a catchy title, the book must still be well written.

Many Christian nonfiction books are a result of the writer's desire to tell the story God gave them. Denny makes the distinction that, while it may be okay to have your personal story woven into the book, the book itself should not be an autobiography. He points out that God has worked in his own life and taught him a ton of lessons, yet nobody in Boise, Idaho is going to care about any of that because they do not know him. Therefore, the writer's challenge is to perfect the craft of illustrating God's truths without just telling your personal story. The only time this is not the case is if you are already a public name or the story you are sharing is newsworthy or pertains to a certain aspect of a current event.

One interesting thought Denny offers is to consider whether your book idea might be better as an article. One way to tell this is if the first one or two chapters are great, but then the book seems to lose steam. He points out that good writing is a challenge and it takes time. He recommends reading the work of good writers and uses Phillip Yancey as a good example, noting that his writing is tight—he does not waste words.

Above all, Denny maintains that writing is a calling from God and that a writer is serving God whether she writes an article that 300,000 people read or a bestseller that one million people read or a church newsletter that twelve people read. As long as it blesses people and is used by God, it is no less a calling. The reality is that writing that bestseller is probably not going to happen. Even Max Lucado's first book did not originally make the bestseller list! In our ego-driven society, we think that numbers matter. But if you are fulfilling the will of God in your writing, then you are a success.

Denny Boultinghouse lived in a number of states while growing up and, as an adult, did full-time ministry in the Central Valley of California. He graduated from Memphis State University in 1972. His favorite styles of music include "the blues" and Austin music. Some of his favorite places include Maui, London, La Jolla, and Pt. Lobos State Park (just south of Carmel, CA). His favorite writers are a diverse lot including: Eric Hoffer, Richard Goodwin, Molly Ivins, Cal Thomas, Jim McGuiggan, Philip Yancey, Tony Campolo, and Brennan Manning. He and his bride have been married for over 33 years and have a daughter who is an attorney in California and a son who recently graduated from Louisiana Tech. He has been employed at Howard Publishing for over twenty years where he continues to be "the most fun person at Howard Publishing."

Meeting Needs

Read Matthew 14:15-16 (Repeated in Mark 6:35-37, Luke 9:12-14, and John 6:5-7)

In this well-known account from the Bible, Jesus feeds the 5000. Interestingly, this was not the disciples' original plan. Because they dealt in the limitations of the world, their first response to the hungry crowd was to send them away to find food. But Jesus saw beyond the here and now and knew what He would do (John 6:6). To challenge His disciples, He told them not to send the crowds away but to feed them. Once again, they responded based only on what they could see: enough food for all those people would cost them eight months' wages. What was Jesus asking of them?

Jesus looked beyond the money, beyond the hungry faces in the crowd, straight into their hearts. He knew that if they left to find food, He might not have a chance to minister to them again. He knew that if they went out into the world to get their physical needs met, they would more than likely allow their spiritual needs to be met by the world as well. Jesus was not going to let a golden opportunity for ministry pass Him by.

Do we allow our limitations and circumstances to distract us from the very real needs around us? People are hungry for more than just physical food, and Jesus knew that. Yet He did not discount the reality of their physical needs either. We should follow Jesus' example and make every effort to provide for physical needs, a key that opens the door of ministry. Just as Jesus proved, we don't need a lot of money, just a willingness to take what we have, offer it up to God and wait for the miracles to follow.

Is there a physical need you can think of that you are capable of meeting in someone's life? God may want to use you to meet someone's basic physical need so that you will have their attention spiritually. Make a plan of action so that that person doesn't have to go to the world to have their needs met. Remember to write about the experiences you have so that others can be inspired to take action as well.

*Inspired by a message given by Rick Warren in his "40 Days of Community" video series.

Becoming a Writing Vessel

By: Rachel Scott

God had a big surprise for me. Like all who follow the Lord, I have been on my own personal journey with God. I did not know that this journey would involve writing books, for this was never in my thoughts. But I believe that God had an important plan and a specific purpose for me to discover, as He has for many of you, which was to find my calling in writing.

I accepted Jesus Christ as my Savior and Lord when I was quite small and was not aware that I had books inside of me. Several years ago a series of events led me to do some Biblical research and I felt compelled to write about the things that God had revealed to me. As others read my work, they encouraged me to realize that I had been given the gift of writing. I just released my first book called, *Birthing God's Mighty Warriors,* and it has been in high demand. This is quite exciting for me!

I believe that God has chosen many people, especially women, in this hour, to come forth with anointed information for the Body of Christ. For God's people to survive in these last days, we are going to need to hear from many who share their love for God through the written word.

God has been preparing numerous people in His army to share in this way. If you are feeling as if you may be one whom God has prepared, then you may want to seek God on several important points.

The first one is **motivation.** Why do you want to write? Anyone can write a story. We learn how to do that in elementary school. But are you *called by God* to be a writer? The Christian bookstores seem to be full of topical books that seem to say basically *the same thing*. This is not necessarily a bad thing. Sometimes a truth must be said in many different ways in order for individuals to gain a proper understanding of it. Various books on the same subjects, do accomplish this task. The one thing that seems to separate these general books from a great one is *anointing*. The *anointing* is a gift. I believe this is where one must seek God. You must ask yourself, do I want to write a book because it looks like it would be a fun thing to do? Do you hope that if you write a best seller, that it could lead to you being up on stage speaking? What is your motivation for desiring to be up on stage speaking? Is it because you want others to notice your hair and makeup and you think it might be neat to be on videotape or TV?

A woman needs to examine her heart and her motives. If this is a *dream of yours* then you must ask God if it is truly a dream from Him or one that you decided was right for you. Those whom God has called to be *anointed* must be birthed out of the heart of God in order for their message to be effective; whether the message is to be written or spoken or both. We can always go through the motions. I want to caution you to seek God for your real motivation. Many times the one whom God has chosen is the one who is hesitant. We see this throughout the Bible as Moses was hesitant (Exodus 3:11-12), Gideon was hesitant (Judges 6:14-16), and many of the prophets were hesitant.

Have I been called? I have been a believer for almost forty years now and during my walk I have seen countless individuals doing things because they thought that God wanted them to, but their actions appeared to be for the wrong reasons. I can not judge their hearts but I have watched while these individuals tried to knock others *"out of the way"* so that they could *"serve God"* through their performance in some form of ministry. If you have to be concerned with other women competing with you, then this should be your first red flag to use to examine your motivation for why you think you have a message to share. *We are all in this great end time battle together.* We all need each other. We need each woman to find her calling and to be content in her place. Too many times, a woman wants what God has given to another woman and the enemy uses this covetous attitude to counterfeit her giftings so she is not effective where God wants to place her. The Bible speaks of our works going through the fire (1 Corinthians 3:13). These carnal works will burn up! (1 Corinthians 3:15). They will not last, nor will they be blessed of the Lord. So, the first great question to ask yourself is: have you been called by God to write?

Another thing to consider is **what are you going to write about?** If you think that you have the calling to write and the gift to write, then do not be afraid to write about what God is saying to you especially if it is something that no one else has tackled. A truly gifted writer will stand out and will be on the cutting edge. Once you begin to see what God is doing with your writings (i.e.: book, newsletter ministry, booklet, tracts, magazine articles, etc.), then you can pray about whether you should seek a publisher and/or self publish. When my book was ready, God led me to self publish because there was an urgency to my message and there was already a Christian market waiting for what I had to say. If you are going to write about homeschooling, motherhood, a Bible study, a cookbook, parenting, etc., then these are areas where others are already interested in your topics and you will be able to find people to purchase your books. Remember that, if you are led to self-publish, a book with proven sales can be picked up by a large publisher and given new life, if that is God's plan.

The secret is to offer yourself to God as His writing vessel. As you select a topic that is important to you, you will see that your joy will come from becoming a vessel that He can use (2 Corinthians 4:7). Ask Him to speak to you and to give you grace to respond. Tell Him that you are willing to be available when He wants to inspire you and then wait on Him. He may wake you one night at two AM . . . get up and write that inspiration down. Over time, you'll see it all coming together, and the best part will be that it will be *His* way instead of your way. If God is in your writing pursuits, then He will prompt you to write what He wants written and, as time goes by, you will get into His flow. As you gather thoughts and write, you will begin to take on His inspirations and the structure will appear. Once your works are written the way that He wants, then suddenly it will all come together. We never know who God will use. It is our faithfulness as His writing vessels that will allow Him to use us. When we each get into the flow of God for our lives, it is a beautiful thing. If your calling truly is writing, then obedience with that call will bring great joy and will bless all of those who cross your path.

> But we have this treasure in earthen vessels to show that this all-surpassing power comes from God and not from us!
>
> —2 Corinthians 4:7

Rachel Scott is the mother of eight children and lives in Windermere, Florida. Rachel is the author of *Birthing God's Mighty Warriors,* which encourages others to consider birthing additional children. She is presently doing research for her next book and is a very powerful and convicting speaker.

Dealing With Jealousy

Read Romans 13:13, I Corinthians 3:3

Now read Romans 12:15-16, Galatians 6:2-5

One of the writers interviewed for this book frankly and honestly discussed how difficult it has been for her to see some of the writers she started out going to writers' conferences with go on to make it "big" in the publishing world.

It is easy to fall victim to feelings of jealousy, especially as you see others succeed and advance while you seem to be at a standstill. Maybe you are a better writer. Maybe you have more training, while a friend just seems to have beginner's luck. This can be hard to swallow. But while instantaneous, fleeting jealousy is a normal human reaction, we should not allow it to fester and take root in our hearts. Jealousy that has taken root becomes a heart attitude. We begin to feel that God owes us and become resentful that we can't seem to catch a break. As these attitudes manifest themselves in our behavior, we are likely to become bitter, angry people that God can't use because our hearts are "far from Him" (Matthew 15:8).

Thankfully, there is an antidote to jealousy. But I will warn you, it isn't easy to do. Take the person that you struggle with feeling jealous towards and celebrate their success. Write them a congratulatory note. Call them and tell them how proud you are of them. Send flowers or take them to dinner. Do this as often as it takes. Slowly but surely, these actions will replace the negative feelings you have been harboring for that person. Allow God to take your obedience before Him and transform it to a heart full of love for that person.

Don't let jealousy take root in your heart. List anyone God brings to mind that you may be struggling with right now. Be completely honest before God. List some specific action steps that you will take this week to celebrate and encourage that person.

*Inspired by a message given by Andy Stanley, CBA '04 Sunday morning service.

Born to Write

• •

An Interview with
Eva Marie Everson

Eva Marie Everson has been a writer her whole life. "As early as I can remember, I had an urge to put pen to paper," she says. "Even when I couldn't write words, I would scribble. I knew there were thoughts and feelings inside of me that needed to make their way onto paper." As she grew, she was constantly writing little stories. Until one day when she was in the seventh grade, her teacher at school asked the class what they wanted to be when they grew up. One by one, the girls all answered: stewardess, secretary, nurse, teacher, mother. "All were acceptable, expected pursuits for women in my generation," Eva Marie explains. When it was her turn, she proudly announced her intention to write novels one day. She still remembers the class' laughter and the teacher's words to her: "Oh, you can't do that."

"Well," she says now, "I bought it. I kept on writing—I couldn't stop that—but I buried my stories in a drawer and went on to live my life." She became a nurse, got married, and had children. One day her husband asked her about her writing.

"What are you always writing?" he wanted to know. She explained that she wrote little stories. "Can I read some of it?" he asked.

"Oh, I'm not very good," she responded. She did let him read some of her writing and his encouragement bolstered her. She continued to write and often wrote plays for her children's schools. The years went by and before she knew it, her youngest was a sophomore in high school. That year, Eva Marie wrote a long letter to a child she had miscarried years earlier in an effort to work through some of the pain and unresolved feelings from that time. As she always did, she went to put that letter in the box where she kept all of her other writing. But this time was different.

Ten months after she wrote the letter, she felt the Lord whisper to her heart to give the letter to the Praise and Worship pastor at her church. Hesitantly, apologetically, she approached him and did what God prompted. "Though I may have doubted whether I was hearing God's voice, I have learned in life that if what I am hearing sounds ludicrous, it's got to be God. I mean, march around the city seven times and the walls will fall down? That's ludicrous. Hit the rock with a stick and water will come out? That's ludicrous."

God's ludicrous suggestion led to the letter being passed through several channels at church and ultimately led to it being re-written into a play for their drama ministry. After that, the children's drama director asked her to write for children's ministry. "The problem was," she remembers with a laugh, "What I knew about children's ministry you could fit on the head of a pin. But I was so excited for someone to like my writing after all those years, I impulsively said yes." Though Eva Marie did not know it yet, her writing career had just begun.

She says, "After writing for children's ministry for about a year, I was taking a walk one day and I could smell jasmine in bloom. The smell of the jasmine reminded me of the smell of honeysuckle, and I could almost taste the honeysuckle from my childhood in Georgia. A story began to form in my mind about a girl who had, like me, been gone from home for about twenty-five years. She returns home, drawn by the honeysuckle, which represents all her memories of home. I went home that day, sat down and began to write. The first chapter just flowed out of me. I began writing and did not stop until one year later when I typed, 'The End.' I had just written my first book but I did not know the first thing about publishing."

Another year passed. In May of 1999, her church sent her to CLASS as training for Bible classes she was teaching. In July of 1999, she attended her first CBA, armed with a proposal for a simple little book idea. "It was so simple," she says, "I couldn't believe no one had ever thought of it before." Her idea was to interview fifty couples about their marriage proposals, interweave their stories with sonnets and scriptures and finish the book with teaching on the Bride of Christ. The idea had come from a class she had taught on Song of Solomon. Nine days after that CBA, she got the first contract, followed later by a second contract. *True Love* and *One True Vow* were both based on her simple little idea.

At that point, things were going well with her writing. She had landed a two-book deal with a publisher and yet, "Something was not resting within me," she says. During that time she would say the same prayer as she took her daily walk: "Lord, You know the desire of my heart is to serve You with my writing and speaking." Then one day she stopped and prayed a different prayer: "No, Lord. That's not true. The desire of my heart is to serve You, period. If You want me to lay down this Isaac, I will. I love You more than speaking and writing."

Two weeks later, she remembers, the floodgates just seemed to open for both her writing and speaking. Much has happened since then. The novel she had written years before, *Shadow of Dreams* was selected to be the first non-romance fiction novel published by Promise Press, a division of Barbour Books. She has written 2 more books for them. She has edited several collaborations. She just finished a book for Cook Communications, that she co-wrote with her daughter, and a three-book novel series co-written with Linda Evans Shepherd called *The Potluck Club Series*. "My life is busy and full. Even when I am exhausted, I'm happy. I truly love what I do," she says.

Eva Marie is quick to point out God's timing in her writing career. "It was no accident that my youngest was almost a senior in high school before I did anything. I love what I do so much that God knew I would have sacrificed my kids and my home for it. His timing was perfect that I was able to do this after I had raised them." When Eva Marie speaks, she always cringes when she hears women downplay their role as mother by saying they do not have a purpose. She is quick to remind those women that the five women in the genealogy of Christ were noted for *being mothers*. "Everything else will wait," she says. "But you have to remember how vital and precious this time is."

From a little girl scribbling her first thoughts, to a discouraged young woman prevented from doing what she was created to do, to a confident writer certain of her purpose, Eva Marie says now, "It really goes back to that question my seventh grade teacher asked. 'What do you want to be?' Whatever the answer, it's about loving God more than that."

In a matter of a few years, Eva Marie Everson has made an impact on the Christian world by successfully crossing genres and rarely becoming predictable. Since 1999 she has written magazine and e-zine articles and has written, compiled, and edited books of both fiction and nonfiction. As a speaker, Eva Marie has crossed the country numerous times, speaking at churches, women's retreats & conferences, and writer's conferences and workshops.

Choosing God Over Our Dreams

Read Galatians 6:9, Romans 14:12
Now read 1 Chronicles 28:10-12, 29:1-13
Finally, read Numbers 20:12, Deuteronomy 34:1-5

In the scriptures for today, we get a glimpse of two men who were God's servants. One spoke face to face with God (Exodus 33:11, Numbers 12:8) and one God called "a man after His own heart" (1 Samuel 13:14). And yet, both men died without seeing their dreams fulfilled. David never got to build the temple. Moses never got to lead the Israelites into the Promised Land. And yet, neither man seemed bitter or angry when they had to lay their dreams down. We even see David praising God after he turns over the temple plans to Solomon. How can they let go of their dreams so easily?

I think the answer to this question lies in the hearts of these two men. As they neared the end of their lives, they knew that the answer did not lie in their earthly accomplishments, but in their deeper walk with God. As they took their last breath, they were able to say with Paul, "To live is Christ, but to die is gain" (Philippians 1:21). They learned that their earthly dreams of serving God and ministry were only part of the process God used to draw them close to Himself.

Do you have a dream of serving God? Do you want to proclaim the gospel before thousands? Do you have a desire to plant churches or lead people to Christ through your writing? Whatever your dreams for ministry are, never put the end result ahead of your primary purpose on earth—to love God with all your heart. In the end, Moses and David knew that, while God had certainly used them to accomplish great things, nothing mattered more than seeking Him first.

As soon as you can, get alone before God and spend some time asking Him to reveal to you when or if your accomplishments are taking precedence over your relationship with Him. Remember that publishing can become an idol just like anything else. Don't let Satan distract you into doing more when God may be calling you just to be still before Him.

Water Skiing and Writing

By: Lorrie Flem

When I was a girl, my daddy decided we should take up water skiing. The first time I tried I remember everyone giving me their personal helpful hints. I only retained some of the advice, but it was enough. I was up!

I remember thinking about what Jesus must have felt like walking on water—wow! I sharply reined in my thoughts. "What in the world are you doing? You're daydreaming! Keep your feet together! Keep your arms apart! Lean back! Don't bend your elbows! Bend your knees!" How was I ever going to keep all of this straight? The next time I skied, the suggestions churned around in my mind. Over time I was able to remember each of the steps so that I almost effortlessly popped out of the water. (Okay, my sister Carisa appeared to pop out with little resistance and I . . . well, didn't.) The point is that soon these steps became second nature to me and I no longer had to work so hard to try to remember them.

Working on my magazine "TEACH" has in many ways been like water skiing. At first, each issue was an enormous effort. This crazy idea of a magazine began in the spring of 1997 when I began asking friends what their favorite homemaking magazine was. When I explained what I was looking for, the response was invariably, "That sounds wonderful! Why don't you do it?" This was not at all what I had in mind! I just wanted to subscribe to a publication that would leave me feeling as if I had had a good chat with a friend, a visit that encouraged me to keep traveling the roads that the Lord was leading me down. I wanted to be challenged to continue striving to be the best wife, mother, homemaker, homeschooler, and friend that I could be.

In August we sold our first subscriptions. I was surprised that anyone would actually give me money for something that didn't yet exist, but they did, so I spent the next two months learning that I knew nothing about the computer or publishing. When I attempted to lay out the articles I had gathered, I was bewildered and soon disheartened by the unwillingness of this machine to cooperate. Right when I began to seriously entertain the thought of cutting and pasting, the Lord intervened and introduced me to a single lady with no children who missed the work she used to do for an old newsletter. From the first issue someone else has done the desktop publishing.

Right from the beginning there have been changes and improvements as we have evolved (I refuse to give such a perfectly nice word away to the Darwinists!) into what you see today. One large change was when I helped my three oldest sons begin selling books. After much prayer, we started this with two ideas in mind: the first was to fund the magazine's goal of giving "TEACH" to pastors' and missionaries' wives whose husbands are in full-time ministry and the second was to be a learning vehicle for the boys.

In the beginning the boys did the book ordering, stocking, filling orders, packaging and shipping. They learned so much as a result of this business experience. To name just a few:

- they understand how much money it requires to run a business
- they take good care of their inventory because they own it and have a great respect for how much each thing costs
- they are learning the importance of customer service and prompt attention to details
- they understand that the care and maintenance of supplies has a direct correlation to profit

If you've been telling your children, "Go to college, get good grades and work at a large company until you retire" you may be teaching them to live from paycheck to paycheck. I believe the future will be very different for our children than it was for our parents. That was good advice for the Industrial Age but now that we are in the Information Age our children can't rely on lifetime employment and retirement checks. My daddy taught us to think like business owners. Randy and I have tried to pass that on to our children.

During this time, after much encouragement and prodding, I had begun to write some articles to use in the magazine. This was significant because I never had any aspiration to be a writer. I saw myself as a reluctant publisher and found I was an even more reluctant writer. My writing came about in obedience to the Lord's calling and I was inspired and humbled with the response.

In 1999 I decided to try and write a pamphlet to use as a give-away with a magazine subscription. I have always loved to talk, and having a captive audience that never interrupted or gave any indication of boredom was great! Before I knew it I had accidentally written two books! In the next year we self-published both of them to sell through the magazine. *What's For Dinner, Mom?* Is full of practical ideas on how to minister to your family from the kitchen with specific instructions on bulk cooking along with delicious, easy-to-make recipes, money saving tips, etc. *Welcome Home Daddy* began where the first book ended and it encompasses ways for moms to turn the hours Daddy is home into cherished memories as we expand on ways to minister to your loved ones with more than just food. Now writing is something I cherish. It is an opportunity to reach many ladies at once with the words God has given me a passion to say: "stay home, obey your husband, treasure your children, and take delight in your work within your home."

Since then we have self-published four books, nine pamphlets, and the quarterly magazine. Through it all, the Lord has been my stronghold. If I keep my priorities in order "all these things will be added unto you." My career is being Randy's helpmeet, a mother to our eight sweet children, and running our home. If I make that my first priority I seem to have just enough time to fit in these other things without upsetting the apple cart. If I begin to spend my time on the things without eternal value, the cost to my family is too high. By beginning each day with a simple prayer, "Lord, I am Yours to use as You will today," life just keeps running over with blessings.

When you look at the Greek for "worker at home" you find two root words; Oikos—a dwelling, home or household, and Ergon—to work or be employed. What I find especially interesting is the order. The first root is indicative of what requires my first fruit, my home. The work or employment only comes afterwards.

We often hear of the Proverbs 31 woman and how she worked from home with an eye toward making a profit. However, my favorite picture of her is in verse 25 where it says she smiles at the future. I believe she smiles because her priorities are in order and peace reigns in her home.

Spring 2005 marks "TEACH's" seven-and-a-half years of ministering to mothers at home. Today the water skiing skills are pretty much second nature. Since our youngest one was two last August, this year I accepted many out-of-state speaking invitations for the first time. I would equate this new adventure to slalom skiing. We are still water skiing but the water is new to us. I will hang on tight to my guide rope and He will hold me up, chart our course, and drive the boat. I am just along for the ride.

Lorrie Flem has been the happy rib of Randy for twenty years. They are the exceedingly proud parents of eight always precious and often precocious children. Lorrie has always been prone to talk and as a result she has authored a number of books, is the publisher and editor of "TEACH Magazine" and a monthly e-zine. She speaks nationally and is known for her humorous and gentle words of encouragement to other keepers-of-the-home. For more information, go to *www.teachmagazine.com*.

Leaving A Legacy

Read 2 Corinthians 3:2, Malachi 3:16, Psalm 102:18

I'll never forget some advice I got from a friend one day as I fretted over whether I would ever see my book in print. She challenged me to really think about why I was writing. Did I merely want to see my name in print? Or did I truly have a passion for communicating my unique story? Yes but, I argued, (feeling pretty smug) how will anyone be blessed by my story if no one can read it?

She didn't miss a beat. "Even if your children are the only ones to ever read what you write, think what a godly legacy you are leaving for them. Your writing can be passed down through generations. But first you must stop waiting for a publisher to tell you it has merit and just write. Write it for your children and grandchildren. Think what a treasure it will be to them."

My grandmother died last year, and at her funeral, we all gathered around to read a book she had filled in for my brother just before she got sick. We giggled as we read her recounting of first dates with my grandfather and descriptions of her early life. In the end, we were all crying as we realized what a precious treasure her words now were. It was as if she was still with us, living on in her words. My brother promised to make each of the grandchildren a photocopy of the book so that we could all have one. My grandmother was not a fancy lady with a list of accomplishments after her name. She never published a book or spoke before crowds. She ran a beauty shop out of her home, loved one man all her life, raised three kids and made the best biscuits you ever tasted. Now that she is gone, her words, her memories, are priceless.

So is your story. Even if a publisher never calls, I can guarantee that your loved ones will be begging for just a cheap photocopy of your words someday. You don't have to be a best selling author for that to be true. Leave a legacy with your words so that generations to come will know the great things He hath done.

Do you keep a journal for your children? Do you make scrapbooks? If you were gone tomorrow, would those that you love have something to hang onto that shows who you are and what they meant to you? Remember not to focus all your writing on writing for others.

Intertwined Callings

By: Mary M. Byers

One question transformed my life.

I was sitting in a time management seminar when the presenter asked a profound question. "What is the one thing you would do if you knew you would not fail?" she inquired.

I knew the answer to the question. *Write a book*. It was my heart's desire. Though I knew what I wanted, I didn't know what I wanted to write about or how to make it happen. Regardless, the desire remained tucked quietly in my heart.

A few years later, when I was twenty-five years old, I was newly married and working full-time, wondering about God's purpose for me. At the time, I was fearful I would miss God's call on my life. Daily I wondered about the work He had prepared for me to do during my time on earth. *"What if I miss His call?"* I wondered to myself on more than one occasion. *"What if I get to the end of my life and discover I frittered away my time on earth instead of spending it how God wants me to?"* I worried.

The answers eluded me. Lacking clarity, one day I fell on my knees and begged God to reveal His plans for me. *"What am I supposed to do, Lord?"* I can still hear the answer that came in the stillness after the question: *Write a book*. It was the second time I'd heard this directive.

I don't think it's coincidence that my heart's desire and God's plan for me were the same. Though the message was identical, I still didn't know what I'd write about or how I would make it happen. But I was convinced that a book was in my future.

I started reading magazines and books about writing. I attended writer's conferences. Most importantly, I began to write. But, still, I did not know what to write about.

The answer to that question—what to write about—emerged slowly. It was tied to another question: Should I have children? To be honest, I made the decision not to have kids on four different occasions. Unlike some women, I didn't grow up with a deep desire to have children. This lack of desire worried me. Did it mean I wouldn't make a good mother? I wasn't confident I'd have the patience necessary for mothering. I worried about the state of the world I'd be bringing kids into. Though my own childhood was a good one and I had a fantastic mother, my indecision led me to believe I shouldn't have kids. But it wasn't what God had planned for me. There was no peace after I decided (repeatedly!) not to have children, which made me wonder if my inability to lay the issue to rest meant I had made the wrong decision.

As in previous years, I again begged God for clarity. Prior to leaving for an aerobics class one day, I again knelt beside my bed and prayed for guidance. I asked God to reveal Himself to me. "Is it in your plans for me to have children?" I asked. This time, I heard nothing in response.

As I drove to the gym, I implored God further. "Please don't remain quiet on this issue, Lord." I prayed. "I desperately need your guidance in this area—once and for all." Immediately, it came. A song by artist Kenny Loggins called "The House at Pooh Corner" came on the radio. The words spoke to me and I knew, without a doubt, that God was calling me to motherhood.

I became pregnant and gave birth to my first child when I was thirty-three. I continued to work. But when my second was on the way, my husband and I decided I should leave full-time employment to be more available to the children. It was a difficult decision for me because I loved my work and the people I worked with. I knew the decision was the right one, however, and I bravely made plans to transition from working outside the home to working within it. It's a decision I've never regretted. And it's a decision that enabled me to fulfill God's call on my life.

Without the demands of getting to the office every day, my schedule relaxed. And as it relaxed, I relaxed. In the mornings, before my children awoke, I began to write. Writing cleared my mind and allowed me to examine my life more closely. The more I wrote, the more I began to believe that I did indeed have the ability to write a book. Since I had just been through a major life transition myself, I wrote a proposal for a non-fiction book about navigating transitions. I found a literary agent without much trouble and took this as a good sign. She began her work marketing the manuscript and I patiently waited for a publisher to show interest.

Months passed. Instead of getting offers for the proposal, rejections came in. The more rejection letters I received, the more I began to feel that God wanted me to write a book in the Christian inspirational market rather than the secular market. But the question remained: What should I write about?

I prayed again for guidance. One morning, as I sat at my computer trying to make sense out of a mothering challenge I was facing, the answer came. How about writing for moms? As a mom myself I knew the joys and heartaches that come with the job. A seed was planted and the idea took hold. I sketched out a book focusing on helping moms meet their own needs while caring for their family. I wrote the first three chapters and crafted a proposal. I found another literary agent. And then, again, I waited.

It took another eighteen months for everything to fall together. During that time, I spent many moments questioning God and waiting patiently for an answer. Shortly before Christmas in 2003, my agent called. Harvest House Publishers was interested in the manuscript and he was confident an offer would be forthcoming. More waiting. In the spring, an offer came and I finished writing the manuscript for my book, *The Mother Load: How to Meet Your Own Needs While Caring for Your Family.*

God called me to write and He called me to motherhood. He beautifully knit these callings together, and in so doing, He fulfilled my deepest desire.

He'll do the same for you if you dare to let him.

Mary Byers is the author of *The Mother Load: How to Meet Your Own Needs While Caring for Your Family,* as well as a professional speaker. She presents frequently to associations, corporations and women's groups. Mary and her husband live in Illinois with their two young children.

"If you find that writing is hard, it's because it is hard. It's one of the hardest things that people do."

—William Zinnsser,
On Writing Well,
1990 4th edition.

One Simple Question

Read 1 Corinthians 9:22-23, 1 Thessalonians 2:8, 1 Samuel 12:23

Part of ministry is building relationships. As we reach out in love to those around us, connections are made and barriers are broken down in the process. There are many desperate, lonely, hurting people out there who long for a kind word or gentle touch. They may be the very people you least expect—with the biggest smile and most expensive car. Yet, inside they are crying out for someone to notice their pain. All people want to feel loved, and the need for love knows no social or economic barriers.

One very simple thing we can do to show love is to pray for each other. It takes nothing at all to ask someone a simple question: how can I pray for you? This is usually not a question that people expect to be asked, but most everyone will have an answer. Very few people will say, "My life is perfect." You may even be surprised by the answers you get. Praying for someone promotes a richness and intimacy in a relationship that is not easy to find. Do not discount the value in it, and don't take it lightly if you say you will pray for someone, according to 1 Samuel 12:23. Allow God to take you to a heart level with more people through the ministry of prayer.

Issue a challenge to yourself to ask at least one person how you can pray for them this week. It's even better if that person is someone you don't know very well. Honor your commitment to pray for them. Write about this experience.

A Writer's Journey

• •

By: Sally E. Stuart

Me? A writer? That was the last possible thought on my mind in 1967 when I was a stay-at-home mom with three small children. My only extra-curricular activities revolved around the church and the volunteer work I did there during the week as well as on Sundays. That was also where my sense of frustration originated—frustrated because I was almost the only one willing to volunteer for those extra duties. I began thinking how great it would be if someone else helped once in awhile.

At the time, I had no idea why—I'd never done anything like it before—but I sat down and started writing out my feelings on the portable typewriter I probably hadn't touched since high school. I'd never even thought about becoming a writer. Actually what I ended up writing was a challenge to other mothers entitled, *How Much is Enough*—asking them how much time they should be volunteering at their local church. When I finished it, I showed it to my husband and he suggested I show our pastor. The pastor liked it and encouraged me to send it to our national denominational magazine. No one was more surprised than I was when they accepted it for publication and sent me six dollars. Not much in today's economy, but it bought more in 1967 and was the first money I'd earned on my own since I'd quit work during my first pregnancy.

But more than the money—I was hooked. Here was something I could do in my spare time. (Spare time? That was a joke. I struggled to find those few minutes here and there I could devote to the writing.) Since I was working with kids at church—as well as my own—I went on to write stories and devotions for children's Sunday school take-home papers (still a good market), and then did how-to articles for Sunday school teacher's and children's workers. I sold virtually everything I wrote—being so ignorant of the publishing business that I didn't even realize that was unusual.

The truth is, I just played around with the writing and only worked it into my busy schedule whenever an idea struck. Then, in the early 70s, I heard about a new writers' conference that was being held at a local Christian college. I had never heard of such a thing, but was fascinated, so I signed up. I listened to speaker after speaker, attended the workshops, and learned a lot, but the one, overarching message I came away with was that this writing thing—the thing I had never dreamed of doing—was God's calling on my life.

I realized first that my success at writing was unusual, but was also an indication that this is where God wanted me. If I had not sold that first article, I probably would not have ever written another word. I was awed, but also humbled that He would call me to such an endeavor. I still had no idea where all this was taking me, but I came away from that first conference knowing one thing for certain. If this was what God was calling me to, I had a responsibility to learn all I could about writing for publication and how to become the best writer I could be.

I started by reading every book I could find on writing. I eventually found two secular writing magazines (there weren't any Christian ones at that time), subscribed to both and read them cover to cover every month. I worked at filling my writing reservoir with everything I could find to help me become worthy of the task ahead.

Another thing I learned at that first conference was the value of attending writers' conferences. I attended again the next year and by the third year I was invited to teach a workshop on writing for children. I'm sure the reason they asked me was that I was the only one they could find that had actually sold to the children's market—not because I was qualified or had ever taught such a class before. Of course, there's no better way to learn a subject than to teach it—so I became an expert almost overnight. I was invited back to teach the next year, and by the mid-70s was able to attend a larger conference in California.

By this time I had quit sending just to my denominational periodicals and was having some success with sales to larger Christian magazines. The problem was that I still didn't feel like I knew what I was doing. Specifically, I didn't know what I was doing right, or what the next step was to improving my skills as a writer. I had the sense that I was shooting in the dark and those sales were just lucky shots.

I think it was the second year that I attended the California conference that I went with one primary goal in mind—I wanted someone to answer those questions for me—to tell me what the key to success was and how I could find it. I actually cornered a number of the editors and instructors and asked them my burning questions. Most laughed when they found out I was selling everything I wrote and told me to just keep on doing what I was doing. They meant well, but did little to solve my dilemma. I finally asked a workshop leader who was also a newspaper editor. He took some samples of my writing and brought them back the next day. I'll never forget his words that day: "I'm not sure I can answer your questions, but I can tell you this. You are one of the most talented writers at this conference, and if I were you I'd stay very close to the Lord." That was not the end of my quest for answers, but it reaffirmed the calling that would change my life forever.

The California conference became a favorite and I attended for three years in a row. By the fourth year, I wasn't sure I could afford the expense of going again and decided to stay home. In God's providence, they called and asked me to teach that year. Those two conferences launched a speaking/teaching career at writer's conferences that has spread across the country and spanned the last thirty years.

I went on to write several books, mostly in Christian education, before I put together the first *Christian Writers' Market Guide* twenty years ago. Even that was not my idea originally. God used an editor I was working with to point me in the direction He had planned all along. Since then I've written mostly resources for writers. I know now that all that preparation was not to give me personal glory as a writer, but to prepare me for this task of creating a market guide each year to help other writers spread the Word through their writing. It's been a remarkable journey.

I often ask myself—why me? I was painfully shy as a child, teen, and young wife, so was not the logical choice to become a teacher. I had no talent for writing anything when I was in school and hated those writing projects (I loved math). I never went to college. In fact, there was nothing remarkable about me at all. Looking back I realize that the success came only because I was able to catch and embrace God's vision for my future. God planned the journey—I just did my best to keep in step.

Favorite quote: "This manuscript of yours that has just come back from another editor is a precious package. Don't consider it rejected. Consider that you've addressed it 'to the editor who can appreciate my work' and it has simply come back stamped 'Not at this address.' And just keep looking for the right address."

—Barbara Kingsolver

Sally E. Stuart has been writing for nearly 40 years and has sold 31 books—including twenty editions of the *Christian Writers' Market Guide, Sally Stuart's Guide to Getting Published,* 7 C.E. resource books, a picture book, and western novel. She teaches at writers' conferences nationwide. She's married with three grown children and eight grandchildren.

God Makes It Grow

Read I Corinthians 3:4-9, Acts 18:4-11

You've written a book, spoke before hundreds, shared Christ with an unbelieving neighbor and prayed faithfully for an unsaved family member. All for the cause of Christ. Now what?

You are His servant, tied to His work and His purposes because you believe in the calling placed on your life. You want to further His kingdom. Your heart's cry is to follow Him all the days of your life. You will fulfill His assignments and meet His divine appointments because you love Him. After all, it's the least you can do after what He did for you on the cross. But who are you? What are you? Have you done anything that could not have been done by 1000 others?

God gave you a gift in inviting you to participate in His work, by including you in His plans to change the world, one soul at a time. Why did He ask you? Because He knew you'd say yes. I Samuel 16:7 says, "The Lord does not look at the things man looks at. Man looks at the outward appearance, but the Lord looks at the heart." 2 Chronicles 16:9 says, "The eyes of the Lord range throughout the earth to strengthen those whose hearts are fully committed to Him."

In this book you've read the stories of other servants of God. You've shared in their victories and felt their disappointments. In the end, you've glimpsed their hearts—the part that matters to God. The accomplishments you've read about are not the point of their stories. The point is that everything they do is for the "write" reason. Each of these contributors would tell you that they are nothing special on their own. They may have planted. They may have watered. But God has made their efforts grow, and that has made all the difference.

If you feel led, spend time praying for the contributors profiled in this book, thanking God for their willingness to share their stories and encourage others. Pray that God will multiply your humble efforts in the days to come as you also seek to glorify God with your writing.

Appendix A: How to Write a Book Proposal

. . . .

A book proposal should have four basic components:

1. A title page
2. A proposal letter
3. A chapter outline
4. 2-3 complete chapters

1. **The title page** should include the title, sub-title (if you have one) and your contact information.
2. **The proposal letter** should not be long and rambling. Most publishers suggest that it be no longer than one page in length, so be succinct in your writing. Consider bulleting some of the information to make the letter easier to read. Realize that the proposal letter may be all that the editor will have time to read. The letter is divided into five parts: 1) *Greeting*: Be sure to address the acquisitions editor you are submitting to by name. Do not use "to whom it may concern." Do some research to learn the name of the person you are sending the proposal to. Open the letter by thanking them for taking the time to read and consider your proposal. 2) *Opening*: Your opening sentence should begin with the title of your book, in italics to make it stand out. The first sentence should tell the name of the book and what the book is about in *one sentence*. This sentence should be powerful and grab the attention

of the reader, while explaining your book idea. Your enthusiasm and passion for the project should come through loud and clear. You can also use this paragraph to address any obvious questions an editor might have, and give a few more details about the book. 3) *Specifics:* In this paragraph, you should identify your target audience (example: women age twenty-five to forty-five). If your book could be part of a series, mention that. Address the needs of society that your book meets. Finally, state the word count for your book and the number of chapters. The publisher needs to know this to be able to run expense projections on the cost of producing your book. A good rule of thumb for an average trade paperback is 50,000 words. A longer trade paperback is about 70,000 words, and a shorter, smaller book is usually about 30,000 words. As for the number of chapters, experts recommend no fewer than ten and no more than twenty-eight, generally speaking. 4) *Marketing:* In this paragraph, tell the publisher how you are going to help market this book. Identify specific networks or credentials you have in place that will make your book more visible in the marketplace. This is the time to name ministry contacts, publishing experience, and speaking opportunities. Obviously, if you are just getting started, you won't have much to list. Work on ways to develop your credentials. The marketing paragraph is also a good time to list other books on the market that are similar to yours and why yours is unique. (For more information and help with marketing, see "Appendix C: Marketing Worksheet.") 5) *Closing:* Thank them again for their time. If you had a one-on-one appointment to present your proposal, thank them for that time as well. Tell them that you will look forward to hearing from them and sign your name.

3. **The chapter outline** is an annotated list of each chapter title in order. If you have not written the whole book yet, there is a temptation to waffle on how and where the chapters will be arranged. This is not the place to do that. Take ownership of your book and organize it accordingly. After each chapter title, give a brief description of what that chapter is about.

4. **Two to three complete chapters** will be the last component in your proposal package. If you are writing a non-fiction book, these sample chapters do not have to be in order. Choose the chapters that you feel best represent the work as a whole and your skill as a writer. If, for example, you are proposing a Bible study with your book, be sure to include a sample of the Bible study. If your book is a fiction book, it is recommended that you include the first three chapters of the book in order.

You may add to your proposal, if appropriate:

- Advance praise/endorsements for your book
- Portfolio samples of some of your other work
- A resume or bio sheet
- Any other personal promotional materials you feel are relevant to the project

Remember that your proposal is what will sell your book, so spend time on it. The proposal should be an example of your best work and reflect your professional abilities. This is the time to do your homework! As you are putting your proposal together, go to the Christian bookstore and look at books that are similar to yours. How are they organized? What topics seem to be important to readers? What is selling well, and why? Learn from other authors. An informed writer who is knowledgeable about Christian publishing will go a lot further than those who don't take time to educate themselves.

Appendix B: How to Create a Bio Sheet

· ·

What is a bio sheet, you might ask? The bio sheet goes before you into a church, introducing you and your ministry to the people who are considering you as a speaker. It communicates the message of your ministry while introducing you as a person. This is a lot to accomplish with one piece of paper! A bio sheet provides important information about you and will affect a church or group's perception of you as a speaker. Not having one—or having one that looks thrown together—makes you seem unprepared and will reflect poorly on your presentation. A bio sheet, then, becomes your opportunity to set yourself apart as a speaker and convince a church that you will meet their expectations.

A bio sheet should include the following sections on the front and back of the sheet:

1. **A photo:** This is absolutely necessary. A church or group will be deciding whether you are a good fit, and your photo helps in that decision. They need to put a face with a name. Make sure that your photo matches your personality. If you are more serious and speak on more serious topics, your photo should reflect that. If you are known for your sense of humor and casual demeanor, use a photo that reflects that aspect of your personality. Make sure that your photo actually looks like you, otherwise the church might feel deceived when they meet you. For that reason, glamorous, highly made-up photos are usually not a good choice for a bio sheet. You don't want to look picture-perfect and over-prepared. Choose the photo that best reflects the beauty that God gave you. If your hairstyle or clothing is outdated, consider having someone help you achieve a more updated look for your photo. You can use

either a black and white photo or color, according to your preference. Black and white is timeless and less expensive to reproduce, but color gives a crisp, fresh look to your bio sheet. Above all, make sure you get permission from the photographer to reproduce your photo.

2. **Your passion:** This should be a statement that reflects your passion in about three sentences, more or less. To create this statement, list five to seven words that you feel best describe you as a speaker. These can come from comments from other people who have heard you speak or evaluations you have received on your speaking. Some speakers even use quotes from others in this "passion" section. Using those five to seven words, write three sentences that enthusiastically describe you.

3. **Who are you?** People want to know you as a real person. This is the section where you describe your family life— mother, wife, where you live, your work experience or current position and a few of your credentials. Don't write a laundry list of credentials, just a few carefully selected, pertinent facts like media exposure, published articles, books published, special training completed, or any unique experience (like if you are an Olympic gold medalist, for example).

4. **Inspirational:** This section is an extension of what you wrote in your "passion" section. In this section you make it clear what audiences you most like to address (for example, mothers of young children) and why they would want to listen to you. What qualifies you to speak to this group? Answer this question: if you come to hear me speak, this is what your take-home value is...

5. **Endorsements:** This section is comprised of a few comments from people who have heard you speak. These are meant to be glowing recommendations, not critical comments! List people who have heard you speak and could endorse you. Ask them to contribute a comment for your bio sheet. If you know someone who is a recognized name, it is good to have that person endorse you to add to your credibility. Keep the letters people send you after you speak to use comments from those letters. If a comment was made anonymously, you can include it, but only use one anonymous endorsement on your bio sheet.

6. **Topics:** The "topics" section is usually listed on the back of the sheet, along with the rest of the information below. Don't list out ten topics with descriptions, as this can overwhelm people. Instead, choose three to four topics you really like to speak on and are secure about delivering. Write out a paragraph description of each topic, without giving away all of your message. Make sure you clearly state the take-home value of each message.

7. **Presentation Variety:** In this section, you state whether you are comfortable speaking for one hour or for an entire weekend retreat. Write out a statement that lets them

know what you are available to do. Churches look for conference speakers who can present several messages over the course of a day, retreat leaders who can speak four times in one weekend, and the standard one-hour presentation. By being flexible in your packaging, you can expand your booking potential. Remember that the stories, illustrations and personal experiences you use can usually be woven into other talks, thereby expanding what you can offer.

8. **Contact information:** How can people get in touch with you? Remember that whatever phone number you give out is how a church will contact you, so consider getting a business line to take calls so that you can be professional in your presentation. Also, there is the security issue involved with giving out your home phone. You might also consider getting a PO Box instead of giving out your home address. Of course, both of these options will only be truly necessary once you build up to generating a lot of requests to speak.

Once you have written and proofed your bio sheet, it is time to get it printed. You can have a cost effective laser copy made or you can have a glossy, slick bio sheet printed and put it in a nice presentation folder. If you are a beginning speaker, there is no reason to spend a lot of money on expensive printing, as your bio sheet should also reflect your level of experience. Have fun with your bio sheet and make it a true reflection of you!

Appendix C: Marketing Worksheet

· ·

In most every case, the publishing industry requires that writers be ready and willing to assist the publisher with the marketing of their book. Indeed, a writer who has a platform is more likely to be published than one who doesn't. This worksheet is designed to assist you as a writer in developing and enhancing your marketability. Knowing and keeping a record of this information will help you to be prepared when publishers ask questions. This worksheet is also essential for those writers who choose the self-publishing route.

Marketing Your Book:
Know your target audience. Who is this book written for? Are they male or female? What is their income, profession, interests, etc?

Why will they buy this book? What are their concerns and lifestyle issues? What is their felt need?

Why will a consumer pick up your book when they walk by it? What will their perception of the book be?

What is the takeaway value of this book? What direct benefit will a consumer receive from reading this book? Why do they "need" it?

What are some key features about your book? Is it a series? Is the title especially unique? Does it offer a Bible study? Is the information you present potentially life changing?

What other authors/titles in the Christian market are similar to your book and how is your book better or different?

Marketing Yourself:
What church/denomination are you affiliated with? Are you especially active in your church or community?

What is your faith background? What is your testimony and how does it fit into this project?

List your publishing credits.

Do you have any contacts or affiliations with a specific ministry?

Why are you qualified to write this book?

Does your book deal with any current events or societal issues that are especially newsworthy?

If you are a speaker, list some specific speaking experiences you have had.

How are you received as a speaker? Include letters and comments you have received as feedback from audiences.

Do you have any media contacts or inroads with the media? List local and national possibilities.

Are you willing to do media interviews, book signings, speaking engagements, etc. to promote the book?

List out some possible interview questions that someone in the media could ask you that pertain to your book.

List any specific marketing channels you know of that would be a good fit for your book. Include catalogs, internet resources, bookstore connections, etc.

Appendix D: Writers' Resources

• •

Contributor Mary DeMuth very graciously supplied us with this annotated list of writing resources. I have added a few other resources at the end. Thanks to Mary for taking the time to organize this rather vast and helpful list!

Annotated writer's links
Author Sites

Randy Ingermanson's web page. (**www.rsingermanson.com**) This site offers some great help to beginning and intermediate writers. He includes his snowflake method of organizing prose and also has author links.

Brandilyn Collin's web page. I met Brandilyn at Mount Hermon this year. She taught the Fiction 101 track with Randy Ingermanson. Her notes from that presentation can be found on her site. (Randy has his notes on his page too.) If you'd like to be inspired, click on the heading about her miraculous healing. Wow! **www.brandilyncollins.com**

Hazel Spire's web page. Hazel attends the Dallas Christian Writer's Guild with me and is a fellow member of the Circle of Poets. She writes lovely poetry and has several youth novels out. **www.hazelspire.com**

Deborah Gyapong's web page. Deborah provides a lot of wonderful services on her web site **www.bestwaycommunications.com**. She's one of the best fiction editors I've met.

Particularly of interest is her new motivational/organization technique called Storyboard Your Life.

Jeanne Damoff's web page. I met Jeanne at Mount Hermon, but we've become more acquainted through the Master's Artist circle (see below). Jeanne provides resources for writers, samples of her writing, and a lot of information about brain injury. Just for fun she shares links to her favorite cyber-places, and she's got some great photos on this site as well. **www.jeannedamoff.com**.

Sandra Glahn's web page. (**www.gospelcom.net/kregel/Aspire2/**) Sandra writes about infertility and biomedical issues from a Christian worldview. She's the editor of Dallas Theological Seminary's *Kindred Spirit* and she teaches journalism at the seminary. Glahn has some great writer's helps on this site.

Jan Winebrenner's web page. (**www.intimatefaith.com/**) Jan leads the Dallas Christian Writer's Guild and is the author of numerous books.

Cec Murphey's web site. Cec has written more books than I can shake a stick at! I had the privilege of meeting him this year at Mount Hermon. He's all energy—a fun person to be around. Check out his site at **www.cecilmurphey.com** and be inspired.

Jim Pence's web pages. I got to know Jim when we put a writer's conference together (along with friends Suzanne and Leslie). He's got an amazing heart for prisoners and goes into prisons to do redemptive chalk drawing presentations. You can see some of his drawings at **www.tuppence.org**. Jim is also an accomplished writer with a great suspense book out entitled *Blind Sight*. Visit his writer's site at **www.jamespence.com**.

Shannon Woodward's web site. Shannon and I met online. She taught a magazine article writing track at Mount Hermon. She's got some great information on her site: www.**shannonwoodward.com**.

Rene Gutteridge's web site. I sat with Rene a few times at Mount Hermon this year. I think we were stalking each other! Seriously, she's a genuine gal who's written some well-received novels. Her site is beautiful, one of my favorite author sites. **www.renegutteridge.com**

Shannon Kubiak's web site. I met Shannon as we rode to the airport together. She's got an incredible ministry to teen girls. Click on **www.shannonkubiak.com**.

Wanda Brunstetter's web page. **www.wandabrunstetter.com**.

Writer's Groups and Conferences

Mt. Hermon Christian Writer's Conference. (**www.mounthermon.org/writers**). This is the premier Christian writing conference in the world. If you are serious about your writing career, take the time to attend. It's well worth the investment. It is usually held in April over the Palm Sunday weekend.

The Writer's View. (**www.groups.yahoo.com/group/TheWritersView**) This is an online professional writer's forum. Members and panelists e-mail their views on industry topics. Topics are introduced twice a week. I've learned more about this industry through this group than any other medium.

Circle of Poets. (**www.groups.yahoo.com/group/circle_of_poets**) This is a small Christian poetry group who shares their poetry for edification and critique. It's been great to stretch my poetry arms through this forum.

Dallas Christian Writer's Guild. (**www.dallaschristianwriters.com**) This is the premier Christian writer's group in the Dallas/Fort Worth metroplex. They meet the first Monday of the month from 7:00-9:30 at Prestonwood Baptist Church. The Guild also has a writer's forum: (**www.groups.yahoo.com/group/dallaschristianwriters**)

The Master's Artist Group. A bunch of Christian artists, primarily of the written word, who don't often fit in the mold of "Christian Author." Check them out at **www.groups.yahoo. com/group/the_masters_artist**.

Online Publications

If you are looking for a great online magazine that challenges your heart and encourages you to hone your craft, check out **www.spiritledwriter.com**. I have a piece there about writing in obscurity: **www.spiritledwriter.com/march2004/musings.html**.

Christian Publishing sites

Alive Communications. (**www.alivecommunications.com**) A premier literary agent agency located in Colorado Springs, Colorado.

Christian Booksellers Association. (**www.cbaonline.org**) If you want to know more about the inside of Christian bookselling and retailing, this site is a helpful one. Information about their yearly convention is on this web site as well.

Research and Writing Tools

Lexical FreeNet Connected thesaurus. (**www.lexfn.com**) A wonderful online thesaurus. I've especially enjoyed its antonym feature.

Bible Gateway. (**www.biblegateway.com**) Search for passages in the Bible by entering in a keyword or a verse. Several different translations available.

Crosswalk.com. (**www.crosswalk.com**) Another great place that has a comprehensive search engine for verses (although this one does not have the NIV translation.) This site has everything,—links to Bible study resources, bookstores, profiles, and articles.

InfoPlease-all the knowledge you'll need. (**www.infoplease.com/index.html?link=tmpltop**) A user-friendly site to help any researcher find facts in a flash.

The Internet Public Library. (**www.ipl.org/div/books/index.html**) Another good place for research.

Refdesk.com. (**www.refdesk.com/instant.html**) Like having your own reference librarian at your fingertips. Great for research.

Smithsonian Institute. (**www.si.edu**) A wonderful site with lots of helpful information.

The Phrase finder. (**phrases.shu.ac.uk**) A great thesaurus resource for finding phrases and quotations.

The Library of Congress. (**www.loc.gov**) Another wonderful place for research.

Writer's Information

Christian Writer's Workshop link page. (**www.billyates.com/cww/links.html**) This has plenty of relevant and helpful links for Christian writers.

Writer's Digest. (**www.writersdigest.com**) A great magazine for new to intermediate writers. The web site is full of helpful writerly information from contests to instructions.

Writer's Information Network. (**www.christianwritersinfo.net**) This site is a wonderful resource for writers. Getting a yearly membership entitles you to a free press card and six issues of "The WIN Informer"—a hotbed of trends, contests, advice, and fellowship. This publication is a must-have for any writer, novice or professional.

Christian Writer's tour of the web. (**www.printerideas.com/cwise**) This is quite a comprehensive list to publications, research and guidelines.

Terry Whalin's web site is chock full of almost anything you'd ever want to know about the business and craft of writing. Once there, you won't want to leave. Some of my articles appear there. **www.right-writing.com**

Kelli Standish's Focus on Fiction site is a haven for CBA authors who long to see excellence and artistic merit in today's fiction. Standish posts weekly interviews here with varied novelists with links to their sites. **www.focusonfiction.net**

Business Publication Helps

Vista print. (**www.vistaprint.com**) This is a wonderful place to create professional business publications for a fraction of the cost. We've created business cards, flyers and ministry postcards on this site. You will definitely need a high-speed connection if you want to import graphics or pictures. I've found Vista Print to be quick, efficient, and cost-effective. Be sure you pay the extra two dollars for a proof. They send it to you via e-mail in a PDF format. There, you can print it off and confirm there are no errors (or locate typos). Don't order your product until you have carefully looked over the proof.

Marybeth's Resources:

Recommended Books:

DeMarco-Barrett, Barbara, *Pen On Fire: A Busy Woman's Guide To Igniting the Writer Within*. This book is great for busy moms to read. Using the idea of taking captive every free moment to write, DeMarco-Barrett helps moms carve out time to write and inspires them to pursue their dreams of writing. Her web site is (**www.penonfire.com**). (This is not a Christian book, so I can not vouch for all of its content.)

Strunk and White, *The Elements of Style*. This little book was given to me in college by my technical writing professor. I have kept that copy all these years, and find it to be an excellent reference.

Zinsser, William, *On Writing Well*. Another book from my college days. This was our text in my senior thesis class. I still find it to be one of the best books on writing out there.

Leal, Carmen, *WriterSpeaker.com*. This book is an excellent resource for Christian writers and speakers. Check out her web site as well at **www.writerspeaker.com**.

Northwest Christian Writers Association, *The Write Start: Practical Advice For Successful Writing*. This book is full of wisdom from published writers sharing their tips and advice. A great resource! (**www.nwchristianwriters.org**)

Dean, Athena, *You Can Do It! A Guide to Christian Self-Publishing*. This book shares extensively on the state of the Christian publishing industry, the pitfalls to avoid in self- publishing, and numerous ways to market your book. A must read for anyone considering self-publishing.

Online Resources:

"The Christian Communicator" magazine. This magazine is a must-have for beginning and experienced writers alike, as it covers trends in the marketplace and other items of interest (**www.ACWriters.com**).

Looking for a writer's conference in your area? Check out (**writing.shawguides.com**).

Write His Answer Ministries (**www.writehisanswer.com**)

About Proverbs 31 Ministries

Proverbs 31 Ministries is a non-denominational, non-profit organization that brings God's peace, perspective, and purpose to today's busy woman. Through Jesus Christ, we shed light on God's distinctive design for women and the great responsibilities they have been given. What began in 1992 as a monthly newsletter has now grown into a multifaceted ministry that touches and transforms lives through a daily radio program, a monthly magazine, inspirational speakers, online devotions and communities, and published books and Bible studies. With Proverbs 31:10-31 as a guide, Proverbs 31 Ministries seeks to equip and encourage women in seven key areas of their lives, which we call the **Seven Principles of the Proverbs 31 Woman**.

- *The Proverbs 31 woman reveres Jesus Christ as Lord of her life and pursues an ongoing, personal relationship with Him.*

- *The Proverbs 31 woman loves, honors and respects her husband as the leader of the home.*

- *The Proverbs 31 woman nurtures her children and believes that motherhood is a high calling with the responsibility of shaping and molding the children who will one day define who we are as a nation.*

- *The Proverbs 31 woman is a disciplined and industrious keeper of the home who creates a warm and loving environment for her family and friends.*

- *The Proverbs 31 woman contributes to the financial well-being of her household by being a faithful steward of the time and money God has entrusted her.*

- *The Proverbs 31 woman speaks with wisdom and faithful instruction as she mentors and supports other women, and develops godly friendships.*

- *The Proverbs 31 woman shares the love of Christ by extending her hands to help with the needs in the community.*

The staff and volunteers of Proverbs 31 Ministries offer real-life solutions to women who are striving to maintain life's balance, in spite of today's hectic pace and cultural pull away from godly principles. Wherever a woman may be on her spiritual journey, Proverbs 31 Ministries exists to be a trusted friend who takes her by the hand and walks by her side, leading her one step closer to the heart of God.

To learn more about Proverbs 31 Ministries, visit our website or call our home office.

Proverbs 31 Ministries
616-G Matthews-Mint Hill Road
Matthews, North Carolina 28105
877-P31-HOME (877-731-4663)
www.proverbs31.org

*Bringing God's Peace, Perspective, and
Purpose to Today's Busy Woman*

she speaks

Proverbs 31:26

Do you hunger for the Word of God and long to teach it with authority and excellence?

Is your heart burdened for hurting women?

Is God calling you to a speaking or writing ministry?

Have you been teaching or writing for years but need a time of renewal and replenishment?

If you answered yes to any of the above questions, then *She Speaks*, the annual speakers' and writers' conference held by Proverbs 31 Ministries, might be just for you. Whether you are teaching a Bible study, writing for your church newsletter or even developing a speaking and/or writing ministry, *She Speaks* offers a variety of informative workshops and general sessions that will further build your confidence, sharpen your gifts, strengthen you personally, and impact your ministry. If writing is your passion and calling, our separate writers' track will equip and encourage you on the amazing journey of fulfilling God's plan for your life.

The purpose of the conference is to encourage, train and equip women God is calling to speak and/or write. Whether you are a beginner or more advanced, the conference promises to be life-changing.

To find out more about *She Speaks*, visit Proverbs 31 Ministries on the web at www.proverbs31.org, email lara@proverbs31.org, or call 877-731-4663.

PROVERBS·31
MINISTRIES
616-G Matthews-Mint Hill Rd.
Matthews, NC 28105

Bringing God's Peace, Perspective, and Purpose to Today's Busy Woman

ABOUT WINEPRESS PUBLISHING

WinePress has been in business since 1991, the result of a successful self-publishing experience. Since that time, WinePress has grown into a group of companies serving Christian writers and speakers around the globe.

Our services include:

- ► Custom book publishing
- ► Industry level editing and book design
- ► Permissions, ISBN # and Copyrighting
- ► Warehousing and order fulfillment services
- ► Distribution to both general market & Christian bookstores
- ► Publicity and marketing
- ► On Demand book publishing
- ► Marketing materials
- ► Web design & hosting

I can't say enough good things about WinePress. If you're looking to break in to Christian publishing, prove yourself and the marketability of your message by self-publishing with WinePress first. Partnering with WinePress got my message into print quickly, enabling me to not only establish a ministry platform for sharing the Gospel with new moms, but also build credibility as a writer.

Rebecca Ingram Powell
Author, *Baby Boot Camp* and *Wise Up! Experience the Power of Proverbs*
Monthly columnist, *ParentLife* magazine

In an industry where subsidy-publishing used to have a negative connotation, it was WinePress that brought the quality and professionalism to the job that gives it its current status as a positive and viable option for writers. You can expect a WinePress book to have the same quality and attention to detail that you will find with the best royalty publishers.

Sally E. Stuart
Christian Writers' Market Guide

Sometimes self-publishing is the best alternative for an aspiring writer, and when it is, WinePress is certainly a good choice. Over a number of years I have been impressed with their honesty and their concern for their writers. The writers I know who have used WinePress all speak so positively about their experience.

Denny Boultinghouse
Executive Editor
Howard Publishing

Providing attentive service, quick responses, and honesty are the hallmarks of WinePess Publishing. Self-publishing can make sense for authors in a variety of situations. When I encounter someone in need of a such a publisher, WinePress immediately comes to mind.

Janet Kobobel Grant
Literary Agent
Books & Such

WinePress Publishing . . . the Leader in Quality Self-Publishing
www.winepresspub.com   1-800-326-4674

To order additional copies of

for the
Write Reason

Have your credit card ready and call

Toll Free: (877) 421-READ (7323)

Order online at: www.upwritebooks.com.

Printed in the United States
94509LV00002B/1-44/A